In Memory of Jesus

Michael Morwood

Contents

Foreword

The gospels of Matthew, Mark and Luke relate a scene in which Jesus asks Peter, "Who do you say I am?" The question is there not just for Peter, but for all hearers of the gospels to answer.

Writing more than thirty years after Jesus' death, the gospel authors provided Peter with an answer that would have been beyond his grasp while Jesus was alive: Peter declares that Jesus is "The Christ sent from God." It is this revelation, put on Peter's lips, that the authors wanted everyone to comprehend and to proclaim. It is how the Gospel writers wanted Christians to remember and honor Jesus. It is how Jesus has been remembered and honored for two thousand years.

By the time the gospels of Luke and Matthew were written, in the 80's, the "Christ" memory extolled the wonderful feats of the divine person who had a miraculous birth, who died for the sins of the world, who rose from the dead, who reconnected "fallen", sinful humanity with God, who opened the gates of heaven, who sent the Spirit of God down to earth, who enabled his followers to become children of God, and who was the heavenly judge of all people.

At the time of this scene in the gospels Peter knew nothing of that Jesus. In the years before the "Christ" awareness dawned on the Christian community, Peter and everyone else who knew Jesus personally would have remembered

Jesus quite differently. The achievements for which the Christ came to be acclaimed would not have featured when Peter and the other apostles and the people who had known Jesus gathered to remember him in the weeks and months after his death.

The story of Pentecost has conveyed the false impression that several weeks after Jesus died a new religion started, with full awareness of Jesus as the "Christ". The reality was that none of the apostles, including Paul who died thirty years after Jesus, became members of a new religion, and that the "Christ" awareness surfaced from reflection and preaching and understanding years after Jesus died. The story of Pentecost is myth, constructed in light of that awareness.

The reality of the early years after Jesus' death was that men and women faithful to their Jewish religion met to keep the memory of Jesus alive and to pledge their willingness to put his teaching into practice.

Their remembrance would have highlighted the man, his beliefs, his readiness to die for his beliefs and his appeal to them to keep alive his dream of establishing the kingdom of God on earth. It would have been accompanied by a deepening conviction that death was not the end of Jesus and that "the Spirit of the Lord" that had moved so visibly in him was now stirring and active in them.

So, how *would* Jesus have wanted to be remembered?

It is my conviction that the Christian religion has remembered and honored Jesus wrongly for two thousand years. It has focused on him in terms of the Christ who overcame disconnection from a heavenly God who withheld forgiveness for human sin and who refused access to himself in his heavenly abode.

The Jesus whom Peter listened to day after day had no such focus. In keeping with his Jewish roots and in fidelity to the movement of the "Spirit of the Lord" upon him, Jesus' concern was with the state of this world and with people not knowing a forgiving God present to them in their every-day living and loving. He was driven by the urgent need for humanity to radically change from the destructive, divisive attitudes and practices that violated the Jewish belief that all people are created in the image of God. He urged his follow-ers to give witness to God's presence within and among them by being neighbor to all. Jesus' message about the *here and now* is one that the world needs to hear today. This is why and how and for what Jesus should be remembered. Yet the religion that professes to remember and honor Jesus has rarely in its long history been ready to risk its survival, as Jesus was ready to risk his, in fearlessly and uncompromisingly demanding a social and political order based on Jesus' teaching. Instead, it has traditionally been more concerned with the next life and with controlling how people gain access to it.

Most Christians know a great deal about Jesus Christ the Savior. Relatively few know the Jesus that Peter accom-panied around Galilee and elsewhere. To know that Jesus requires imagination and the effort to explore what might have been the human reality of the man and his dream.

In Memory of Jesus is a mixture of imagination, fact and autobiography.

Part One is a conversation between Jesus and his prison guard the night before Jesus died. While purely imaginary, it provides a context for Jesus to explain his life's work and to state how he wished to be remembered.

Part Two is a brief historical note.

The historical context is important for the conversation in Part Three between two followers of Jesus about forty years after he died. The conversation, again imaginary, pro-vides an understanding of how the remembrance of Jesus changed radically, split the followers of Jesus, and shaped the future of Christianity.

Part Four is autobiographical. It is my journey from being a conservative Catholic who knew and accepted unquestioningly the Church's theology *about* Jesus as Savior of the world to someone who slowly came to *know* Jesus as friend and companion - and who had most of his theological beliefs turned upside down in the process.

Part Five is another conversation, this time between me and the Jesus I've come to know. We talk about issues facing religion and the world today. Obviously, I am putting words onto Jesus' lips, but this is the Jesus I have come to know, and the conversation is real for me. Isn't this how the authors of John's gospel came to compose Jesus' long speeches in that gospel? This conversation is intended to show how I believe Jesus would want to be remembered and how I believe rightful remembrance of him would make the Christian religion more relevant and helpful for humanity than it is today for many people.

Michael Morwood
Easter 2014

PART 1

Jesus and Tim

"Shalom... Are you awake?"

"Shalom... Yes, barely. Where am I?"

"You're in the cell below Caiphas' house. You were beaten up rather badly by the temple guards a while ago then carried down here."

"Oh..."

"Some of the temple priests had a meeting with you before that. Do you remember it?"

"Ah... yes. I remember it ... and the beating."

"I'm sorry about what happened to you. It's not the usual way of putting someone on trial. It all seemed rather hurried and spontaneous. You must have made some powerful enemies around here for this to happen the way it did... You are Jesus, aren't you?"

"Yes. How do you know my name?"

"I think everyone in Jerusalem knows your name after this past week.

"People are still laughing at the way you upset Pilot's grand entrance into the city with your entrance on a donkey. You upset the temple leaders with your dramatic behavior in the temple during the week. Now the priests have had you beaten half dead. Do you have a death wish or something?"

"No. I don't want to die, but if I do die, I want people to notice it."

"Well, you've achieved that..."

"Would you like some water? I'm not supposed to offer prisoners anything, but at this hour of night no one is around to notice."

"Please."

....

"Here's the water. I'll open the door and come in. I'm not supposed to do this either, but I think I'm safe with you."

...

"Thank you. Thank you. What's your name?"

"People call me Tim."

"Thank you, Tim."

"Would you like me to stay in here with you, or would you rather rest and try to sleep."

"I'm feeling too much pain to sleep. Please stay and keep me company."

"Do you want to talk, or should I just sit here quietly?"

"Oh, please talk. It'll take my mind off the pain."

"I'm not much of a talker, but I am a good listener and I have many questions about you. But I don't want to bother you with them if it hurts you to talk."

"Oh, it doesn't hurt to talk. And I probably need to clear my mind. Responding to your questions might help me do that."

"People say they have never known you to be unkind or to speak ill of anyone. Some say you are a prophet. I know you are also a healer. Do you see yourself as someone special?"

"That's an interesting question. 'Special'? Yes, I believe so, but I also believe that everyone is special in the way I think I am. It's just that most people don't realize it."

"*Everyone* is special? In what way?"

"I believe everyone has the Spirit of our God within them. It's part of who we are. We are created in God's image. That makes everyone of us special. Sometimes we have a deep sense of that Spirit within us and allow it to move us to love and live justly. Other times, maybe most of the time for most people, their awareness of the Spirit is deadened by what they believe, so they have no sense at all of being special."

"But that's not the case with you? You have this sense of God's Spirit in you?"

"Yes. It's something I've always had. It started when I was a young boy. I was fascinated by the fields and the animals. I had a sense of wonder about life. I was captivated by the buds of new life and the growth that occurred after everything seemed to have died. I was delighted by the richness and vitality of the natural world around me. I sensed God's Spirit in the beauty and continuity of it all. I also knew other children who shared this same sense of delight.

"But it was more than sensing God's presence in nature. The goodness and spontaneous kindness I saw in people around me, in my family and relatives and other people in our village made a deep impact on me. While I was still quite young I came to a profound conviction that God's presence was in this goodness. I found it natural to believe that if we are created in God's image and if we believe that God is good, caring and compassionate then the goodness, care and compassion I saw and experienced around me were expressions of God's presence. It seemed obvious to me. As a child I delighted in sensing that God was so close to me. This powerful awareness shaped my life in ways I could not have imagined. I often encouraged people to recapture their childhood sense of delight and openness to God's presence.

"What troubled me in the years after childhood was the discovery that most adults thought of God as distant, remote and controlling. It's hard to put into words, but I thought of God not only as Someone - I generally addressed God as 'Father' - but also as a Presence all around me. I sensed God's presence holding everything in existence, putting life into every living thing. Because I believed that God was connected with everyone and everything I had no problem thinking that God's presence was in me and in everyone else. I've always felt it as a sense of overwhelming benevolence and kindness, a wondrous experience of graciousness."

"As I look at my life and the suffering all around me, I wonder whether God has abandoned us. I don't see any of the benevolence and graciousness you just mentioned."

"Why don't we see it? Is it God's fault? Is the Spirit of God no longer with us? Has God stopped being gracious and compassionate? No, the God I knew as a child and now as an adult is still here with us. God has not abandoned us. The fault lies in people refusing to let the Spirit of goodness and benevolence influence their actions. Look at the political, social and religious systems we live under. We see violence and fear and intimidation and hopelessness everywhere. This is all created by humans mistreating one another and silencing the inner voice of God's Spirit that urges us to act otherwise."

"Maybe, but we can't change the way things are. What are we to do? Drive the Romans out of Jerusalem?"

"Oh, it's not just the Romans. We have to see well beyond them because their time of domination will come to an end one day. We need to make sure their unjust and brutal methods will be replaced by something far better. That is our responsibility, and we don't have to wait until the Romans have gone. We can start with what's going on right here in the temple. We need to change the way people think about God, the way they think about themselves and how they think about other people."

"You're a bit of a dreamer, eh?"

"Well, it's not just my dream. Isn't the dream of a better world the dream of our Jewish faith? Isn't this precisely what we Jews have always expected and longed for? Isn't this what our Covenant with God is meant to produce, that we would live God-conscious by our respect for the Torah and create a society characterized by justice, compassion and peace?"

"Yes, that's true, but God doesn't seem to be helping us much these days."

"God, God, God … there you have it. We're always waiting for God to do something. We want God to act. When are we going to understand that *we* have the Spirit, the impulse of God, within us and that we are supposed to use this power in us to create a better society? The problem is not with God. The problem is that we Jews have not understood that the Spirit of God acts in and through us. We have to believe the Spirit is within and among us. *We* have to do the work if the Kingdom of God is to become a reality. Our Scriptures make it clear what God wants of us and how we are to do it. How *we* are to do it is the issue."

"That's a tall order. We can't change the way our religion works or how the world is ruled. Take me, for example. I can't do much at all, except to keep the Law, to look after my family, not to cause any trouble and to make sure I safeguard my work here as a guard. I don't think it's my role or even within my capability to change how society operates."

"You reflect the sense of powerlessness of most good-living people I've met. People have become passive and dependent. They are lost. They are like sheep without shepherds to lead them to pastures that will nourish and sustain them. Look at what goes on in the temple. The religious authorities lord it over people, keeping them in control, and instilling fear of punishment if they disobey. They also make sure not to upset the rich and the powerful. Here in Jerusalem our religion has become a business. It has lost all sense of direction. It fails to inspire people to believe that God's Spirit is with them and to have confidence in the promptings of that Spirit. It's much easier and far more convenient for our religious authorities to demand peoples' blind obedience rather than to empower them through belief in God's presence with them. This is not the first time in our history that our religious leaders have failed in their duty. We all know how at different times in the past our prophets steadfastly rebuked the behavior of the leaders in our religion."

"Have you been trying to turn people against our religion? Is this why you were arrested tonight?"

"No, no. I don't want to do that. I am a faithful Jew. What I want to do is remind people why our religion really exists. Its purpose is to help us to create God's reign on earth. I love and respect my religion. I just want it to do what it should be doing. It should be giving hope to people, not driving them more and more into a sense of hopelessness and powerlessness. That's not what our religion is about. It should be empowering people to do God's work on earth."

"You sound passionate about this. When did you first start talking to people about the way you see things?"

"Oh, I started young! I can remember having lively discussions at our evening meals when I was that young boy filled with a sense of God's presence. I would ask my parents and relatives why we had the Torah or why we thought God punished people by afflicting them with blindness or leprosy or why people thought God had abandoned them. When I was a little older I began to question our synagogue leaders the same way. I was keen to discover why adults did not think the way I did."

"And what did you discover?"

"Just what I mentioned a moment ago, that our religion does not sufficiently promote the long-held Jewish belief that we are created in God's image. It neither affirms the dignity of that truth nor calls people to live it out in their daily lives. Instead it seems intent on trying to suppress any personal belief that people carry God's powerful Spirit within them. It disempowers people and leaves them thinking they have nothing to offer except to do what they are told."

"So at some time in your life you decided to empower people? No wonder you are considered dangerous!"

"I knew I'd be treading on dangerous ground. I held back for some years, not sure of where and how to start. But there was an irresistible urge from deep within me to do something. I came to understand what it must have been like for the prophets when they felt compelled to step forward and speak God's message. It's not as if God spoke to me from heaven or anything like that. It came from inside me, a part of me, prompting, suggesting, pushing, yes, *pushing* me. There came a time when I knew that I could not *not* follow this insistent inner urge.

"So I waited, watching for some sort of sign, I guess. Then I heard about my cousin, John. You probably heard about him as the baptizer who was murdered by Herod. I went to the Jordan River to see him and it was there I made my decision to make empowering people with a sense of God's presence my life's work."

"Yes, everyone knew about John and we all know how he died. But if he was your cousin and you went to see him, why didn't you stay and work with him?"

"I was inclined to do so at first, but I came to realize that we had a different message to preach. John was more concerned with people changing their lives in order to be ready for God's activity. He preached about *'God's angry judgment'*. That was not the message welling up inside me. I've never thought of God as angry, despite what our Scriptures say. My sense has always been that God is not going to get angry and act in some decisive way as our story about the exile in Babylon suggests. I've never believed that God is like that.

John's preaching did not empower people. It frightened them into changing how they behaved - for a short time. My time with John deepened my conviction that God is not going to intervene to repair the bad situation we find ourselves in; we have to do it, and we will never do it unless we find some way of believing we can do it."

"I guess that means you were not baptized by John?"

"Oh, yes, I was. As I sat by the river, watching and reflecting on what was going on, I realized this was my stand-up-and-be-counted moment. I decided that if and when I walked into the river and asked John to pour water over me, it would ritualize my determination to allow God's Spirit within me to lead me wherever it would. So when I approached John, I fully understood the consequences of my action."

"Did John know you disagreed with his preaching?"

"Yes, but it didn't concern him. In fact, he even said he thought I was taking on a greater and harder task than he, and wished me well."

"You're shivering. Here, let me put my coat around you."

"You're not supposed to do that, either, I'm sure…

"Thank you. Are you here every night?"

"No. I'm summoned here only if anyone is to be held overnight. None of the temple guards like staying here all night by themselves. This is unexpected. I was in bed when the caller came tonight and I had no idea you were the prisoner until I arrived. I was deeply shocked to find you in such a state. Did you have any idea you would end up like this?"

"Like you, I know our Scriptures. Isn't this the treatment most of our prophets received? Yes, I knew there would be serious opposition and even persecution, but I was naïve enough to believe that the message I had would inspire and empower people and would bring about the change I longed to see."

"You really believed that!"

"Yes. It's what drove me. I remember an early visit to my first home village of Nazareth after meeting with John. The text at the synagogue was from Isaiah where the prophet declared, *'The Spirit of the Lord God is upon me. The Lord has anointed me to bring good tidings to the afflicted.'* I'm sure you know the rest of that passage. I had a clear realization, yes, that's me. I have a message of good news, a way to set people free from whatever enslaves them into thinking they are of little worth and have nothing to offer."

"Anointed? How do you know you are anointed by the Lord?"

"It's not as if God actually spoke to me or that anyone physically anointed me with oil. As I said earlier, a call came from deep within me. I knew in my mind and in my heart that this was what life was asking of me. I identified the call with God's Spirit asking something of me. I think all our prophets must have had a similar experience."

"You said earlier that everyone has the Spirit of the Lord God within them. Does that mean we are all anointed by God in the way you believe you have been?"

"Yes. We are *all* anointed by the Lord God. We are all created in God's image. The Breath, the Spirit, the Life of God is within everyone. It moves differently in each person, so we should each hear a call from within us to give expression to the Spirit in the best way each of us is able. The fact that I feel myself moved by the Spirit in a way that you do not doesn't mean I have the Spirit and you don't. The critical issue is that most people don't realize that this wonderful, powerful, creative Spirit of the Lord is within them, or is *'upon'* them as the text from Isaiah says. That's what I wanted to address."

"You have healed people of leprosy and blindness and all sorts of ailments. How are you able to do that and I can't?"

"I don't have an easy answer to that question, but I do think it is connected with my belief that God can work miracles through us. That almost drove some of my disciples crazy because when they tried to have the faith in God I asked them to have, and attempted to heal people, it didn't work. I would add that in some people the ability to heal is connected in some way with fasting and prayer. But I'm most inclined to think it's a gift. You can't make it happen. I think it's similar to the fact that some people can sing well, while others can't hold a tune. Healing is God's doing; not mine. All thanks must go to God. Also, the people being healed must have some faith in God. I've never been able to heal anyone who did not believe God could do this through me."

"Did you ever meet such people?"

"Oh, you should have been in Nazareth during one of my last visits there! Not only did the people not believe, they drove me out of town! It was inconceivable to them that the son of a Nazarene carpenter could heal people. They were convinced I was up to no good. It was a most unpleasant and upsetting experience. It took me some days to get over it."

"It must be wonderful to be able to heal people."

"I find it all so strange, really. On the one hand, it's a humbling experience being so closely connected with God's power at work, and seeing what that power can achieve. On the other hand, it's perplexing. People see someone healed of leprosy, for example, and they rejoice momentarily. They hail me as a healer, but they don't think about it enough. They don't see beyond the cure. They fail to recognize the presence and power of God at work here, now, in the community. I always try to link the two because I believe that the healing itself and faith in the presence of God's Spirit are interconnected. I long for people to see and understand what was happening in the way I see and understand it, but most people don't grasp the message. They just see something out of the ordinary."

"What was your first experience of healing someone?"

"I remember the day well. After choosing some men to be my companions I returned to Capernaum where I was living at the time. I was invited to speak in the synagogue and no sooner had I started when a man began to curse and scream. Everyone knew him. They knew he was harmless. However, people generally avoided him because he would start yelling at them if they came too close. When he started to shout in the synagogue I felt a profound sense of closeness with him. It was quite strange. I knew in my heart I could somehow reach into his heart and mind and stop this behavior, and I did. It was simple, really. As I held him I knew that something of the Lord's Spirit in me connected with the Lord's Spirit in him, and he was healed."

"I can imagine that everyone in the synagogue was amazed."

"Well, yes. The story grew and grew. The event was expanded into a grand story about me casting out demons, and the man who had been healed talking about me as '*the holy one from God*'. The story spread all through Galilee!"

"And I suppose the people in Capernaum never gave you a moment's rest after that, wanting you to heal people?"

"Yes. I could have set up a house for healing. I remember going to the house of Peter, one of my companions, after we left the synagogue. His mother-in-law was ill with fever and I was able to restore her to good health. By evening time, it seemed that the town had collected everyone who was sick and brought them to the house."

"But you didn't stay there. What made you move on?"

"I went outside to pray early the next morning and it became clear to me that I had to preach my message and not be known only as a healer. The message was more important.

The healings would hopefully be a sign to people that the Spirit of the Lord was acting and speaking through me."

"Where did you first start to preach?"

"For some time I stayed in Galilee. Here in Jerusalem we Galileans have a reputation for being troublemakers, but we have a lot to be troubled about. When Herod Antipas rebuilt Sepphoris and built Tiberius it caused enormous problems because he raised taxes to pay for the building projects. The local fishermen were hard hit by that and are not likely to recover. Then, there was the increasing population in those two towns, and people had to be fed. In former times that would have helped local small farmers, but unfortunately the land is no longer in their hands. It is now controlled by rich landowners who make the people work hard for little return. Both on the land and on the sea there is injustice and suffering, thanks to the rich and powerful. Galileans have always believed that Galilee is God's own country in a special way. The unjust systems of control are in stark contrast to our dream of what Galilee should be like, so I travelled around my own countryside, trying to give people hope in the midst of oppression."

"How could you give them hope? You had no way of changing the politics or the economic system."

"That's true. But the most hopeless place to be is to think that God is absent or that God is punishing you when the circumstances of life are tough or cruel. I wanted to free people from any belief in a punishing God. I wanted to assure them that the Spirit of God was with them in their everyday lives, however painful and difficult their lives might be. I wanted people to trust in God's presence with them and find hope for the future."

"You mentioned before that you chose some men to help you."

"Yes. I began by inviting a small group of men, fishermen mainly, to be close to me and learn more about what I wanted to do. Twelve seemed to be an appropriate number. I spent a lot of time instructing them and then sent them out as apostles who would spread my message. I wanted everyone to hear my message and I knew I could not do it on my own."

"How did that work out for you?"

"Oh… rather despairingly. I was disappointed, I would have to say. I think it was too much of a turnaround in thinking for them, and too soon for me to expect they would really grasp my message. I think they hoped everything would change suddenly and that they would be doing all sorts of wonderful things. But it doesn't work like that. I think they're still struggling with it all. I hope time and reflection will help them understand what the real issues are."

"Why would you choose uneducated fishermen to help you? Surely you were expecting too much of them."

"I made Capernaum my home village some time ago. I know the area. I know the people. I know their goodness. I saw evidence of God's Spirit acting in them in their way of life and in their care for their neighbors in hard times and in their respect for the sea and the land. What does uneducated really mean? These men and their families lived by values that I wanted to be associated with. I had no hesitation in inviting them to work with me."

"Yet you said they make you despair."

"Yes. They do. But I've come to realize that it takes people a long time to change from deeply ingrained religious beliefs about God, about themselves, and about how religion should operate."

"How did people respond to your preaching? Were you able to get through to them better than your companions?"

"I would have to admit I was often disappointed. I had hoped that my preaching and cures would change peoples' thinking and attitudes but it rarely did.

"This was a big lesson for me. At first I had high hopes that these encounters might spark a change in people. When that didn't happen I realized I had to learn to plant seeds and simply leave them there to develop in their own good time. I had to trust that the seeds would germinate and be nurtured, perhaps long after I had gone. I found that difficult. It meant trusting the future and not seeing the fruits of my own work. But I still believe there will be a harvest one day when my message dawns on people with the help of God's Spirit in their lives."

"What were the seeds you planted?

"I learned the value of story. Leaving people with a story to remember is invaluable. People like stories. They like to retell stories. The more they tell them, the more they will be able to draw out meanings and inferences. There's something about story that is self-educating as people discuss what the story means for them. When I told stories I wanted my listeners to go home and think about what I had said. I told stories about the unexpected, stories designed to help people look at things in a different way. If some of my stories continue to be told, I'm hopeful they will bear fruit one day."

"I know two of your stories. In fact, I think all of my friends know these stories."

"Really! Which stories?"

"One is about the father and his two sons, where the wayward son returns to the father and receives a warm welcome and a big feast while the other son sulks."

"And what do you and your friends think the story is trying to say?"

"Well, we think about each of the characters in the story. We think the story is unfair to the son who stayed home and was loyal, but we don't like his attitude. We think the story is saying that loyalty should go hand in hand with being big-hearted towards people. What's the virtue in being loyal and hardworking if that attitude of heart and mind is not there? We think the wayward son would be changed forever by his father's warm and unexpected reception. We think the father is meant to represent God and that the story wants us to think about God as forgiving and loving. It invites us to be humble, grateful and generous as we imagine the wayward son would have been after he returned home and experienced such love."

"I think maybe I should have chosen you and your friends to be my apostles! So you really do think about and retell the story?"

"Definitely. People like it very much."

"I'm pleased to hear that. What's the other story?"

"It's the story about workers in the vineyard and the latecomers who received the same wage as the men who worked all day. We have some trouble with this story. We like the ending, which we think is about God's extravagant generosity, but there's a problem."

"I think I know what you are going to say, but tell me anyway."

"Well, what happens the next day? No one would work all day. All the workers would come only for the last working hour!"

"Isn't that why the story is effective? It captures attention and makes people think. Yes, the ending is illogical. No one could afford to run a business that way. But while the listeners know that, they also know the story is asking them to ponder something out of the ordinary: that it is the nature of God to be gracious beyond all human reasoning and logic."

"I'd love to hear more of your stories, but I suspect you didn't only tell stories. What else did you say to people as you moved around."

"There were several points I mentioned almost everywhere I went. They all focus on the urgent need for us to take responsibility for bringing to life the heart and soul of our religion, which is to establish God's reign on earth. There is nothing more important than this. What is to be the future of humanity? Is it to be what we experience all around us these days - oppression, domination, violence, fear and hopelessness? We are overwhelmed by all this and we think we can achieve little. Yet, our religion and our Covenant with God has always called us to be like the mustard seed or a light to the nations or a voice for the hopeless and the oppressed. We are called to reject injustice and to work for a better human society. We are never to give in to despair and to accept hopelessness as our lot. We cannot take on the Roman army, but we can ensure that our basic attitude to life is grounded in our Jewish faith and our care for one another and not in despair.

"Almost always, my starting point was the need for my listeners to change the way they thought about God. Such a huge task! At times it seemed as if I was talking to the walls of the synagogue or to the grass beneath my feet. People are so deeply entrenched in images of God they have carried most of their lives. Unfortunately, our Scriptures carry some blame for that. People think of God as distant, as punisher, as judge, as not at all interested in them. Mostly I think they are fearful of God because sickness and pain are all around them, and they think this is all part of God's judgment and punishment on them. Or they think that God wants them to bear hardships for some reason or other. People have been taught to believe that they are sinners, so they have no personal experience of our great religious commandment. How can you love the Lord God with all your heart and all your soul if you are fearful of God and have no personal experience of God loving you? That's an enormous difficulty for people to overcome."

"So, how did you try to help them overcome that difficulty?"

"I tried to engage their imagination and their thinking by using images from their everyday experience. As with the stories I told, I gave them images and invited them to go home and think about the images later. For example, I would ask them to imagine holding a baby and then ask whether they would deliberately drop the baby or wish the baby harm. I would suggest they imagine themselves in relationship with God like a child in the arms of the most loving and caring parent. I asked them to reflect on their love for their child. If we know how to care and love and how to express tenderness, how much more does God? I wanted them to think about their relationship with God and to begin relating with God in the same way they would relate with the most loving father or mother."

"Do you think this was effective?"

"Yes and no. I think many listeners were cynical. I had a sense that they wanted to say to me, 'You should try walking in our shoes, with our pain or sickness, and then see if you would talk on and on about a loving relationship with God'. But, as with the stories, I hope people will think about the image, especially when they hold a child in their arms. It's all about planting seeds and being hopeful."

"What other images did you use?"

"I often used images from nature. I told them to look at flowers and crops and fruit trees and what their beauty and the way they grow can tell us about God's Spirit in the world around us. I wanted people to become aware that this same Spirit that we see active everywhere is in each of us. Whatever is in nature by way of beauty and growth and possibility is in every person. I wanted to open peoples' eyes and minds to that reality. God's Spirit of life and beauty and goodness is in everyone."

"I hear what you are saying, but how do we know that it's not just your pious thinking? How do we get beyond the cynicism you mentioned, which, by the way, I can well understand?"

"Until people see the connection between what they do in their everyday lives and what they hear me saying, it might sound little more than pious words. People have to see and experience for themselves the connection between their everyday experience of being decent and kind and the activity of God's Spirit in them. That's the important point. I want them to recognize that when they are generous, considerate, and forgiving that they are allowing the Spirit of God to be expressed through their love and care.

"Think of all the people you know personally. How many of them are evil people? Very few, if any, I would think. Most people are good and hard-working. They care for their families and they're willing to help others. They try not to harm anyone. If they would only reflect on this reality in their own lives, on their own goodness, they would eventually make the connection I long for them to make. I want them to think, 'Ah, our loving kindness to one another is an expression of God's loving kindness'. Hopefully they would then be able to see a little deeper and come to realize that their many ways of expressing love give expression to the Lord's Spirit within them. That's the really crucial 'Aha!' moment of awareness. It's only then that people will learn to trust that the Lord's Spirit in them can lead them to promote new possibilities for the creation of God's kingdom among us."

"That's very challenging, though. As I'm sitting here listening, I'm thinking this is wonderful and encouraging. Until you get to that last bit and I'm taken back to what I said earlier: Me? You're asking the likes of me to promote these new possibilities for God's kingdom when I am looking at you beaten half to death because of your new possibilities? Do you really expect someone like me to leave whatever comforts I have in life and follow your way of life when this is where it leads?"

"*My* way of life? No, that's not right. It's not my way. It's the Jewish way. If you think I'm wrong or am being too demanding just look at our Scriptures. You know we are called as a people to make God's presence among us evident in all we do. Look around and ask yourself how well we are doing. Look around and ask are there no new possibilities at all for us to be more faithful to our calling to establish God's kingdom of justice, compassion and peace. And stop thinking it's the task of the temple establishment. This is a task in which every Jew must actively participate and in which they must have a voice."

"If all you are doing is telling me and others I must be a better Jew, then why are you here in a prison cell?"

"Religious leadership here in Jerusalem has too much vested interest in working with the Romans and in protecting wealthy business interests. Earlier this week I used Jeremiah's term to describe the temple as '*a den of thieves*', a refuge for the rich and powerful who oppress people. It's a scandal. '*Acting justly*' does not apply in the temple. What's happened to me tonight is no different from what happened to any of the prophets who criticized our religious leadership for taking its eyes off justice and care for the weak. Our leaders don't want to hear about or see anyone empowering people. They don't want people to believe the Spirit in them can establish our Jewish dream of a society based on justice. They certainly don't want to upset the Romans, especially now when so many people are in Jerusalem for Passover."

"And the Romans don't want to hear anyone questioning their rule. That is punishable by crucifixion. This could get really bad for you."

"We'll see what the morning brings."

"Are you afraid to die?"

"I've often wondered how my life would end. Sometimes I hoped that I might die surrounded by friends. That hope died in me not so long ago when I heard how my cousin, John, died. From that moment on, my issue has been whether I would be taken away and locked up as John was, and then die a lonely death, or whether I would meet death head on and die on my own terms. That's why I came to Jerusalem. If I should die soon, I'll at least have the satisfaction, small though it might be, of hoping that I will be remembered as someone who made a statement, by the way he confronted his death, about what he believed. That's the hope I will hold onto in the hours ahead. I'm not afraid to die."

"Do you believe in life after death?"

"I don't know what lies beyond death, but whatever it is, I'm not anxious about it. I know the Greeks and the Romans believe in a journey beyond the here and now to a heavenly place where their gods live, but I don't think our God is removed from us like that. I believe we need to stop thinking about God the way other people think about their gods. God is Spirit, everywhere, *'as far as the east is from the west, and beyond'* as our Scriptures tell us. I've never believed or taught that God is an overseeing, manipulating deity, distant from all of us in our everyday lives. My understanding of

God is more expansive than that. Our Scriptures have some wonderful images to help us: *God is generous beyond measure; God is compassionate and steadfast in love; God's fidelity will last forever; God is always present with us.* When I think about death I put my trust in this understanding. Yes, I've had moments when my belief has been tested by what happened to me, such as being here in this cell, but my basic attitude is to trust that whatever happens beyond death is in the hands of my loving God."

"Most of us tend to believe that whatever happens in our lives is in God's hands. Do you think God wants you to die at the hands of the Romans?"

"I don't believe in a God who wants me to die a cruel death. I mentioned a little while ago that I invited people to think of themselves in relationship with God like a child in the arms of a most loving parent. I cannot think of God in any other way than like a father or mother who dearly loves their child. I refuse to believe in a God who plans and inflicts bad things on people. The situation I am in right now is surely not planned by God. What sort of God would that be? Certainly not my God. No, this is the result of human injustice, and even as I am in the midst of it I refuse to believe that it has anything to do with God wishing me harm."

"Where does God fit in, then?"

"I believe my God is not at all like other gods many people believe in, not even like the God we Jews sometimes think of when we relate our history, a heavenly controller of everything that happens. I believe God is beyond all description, but I believe that words such Breath, Spirit, Love, Compassion and Graciousness, are among the best words we have to talk about what God is like. I've tried so hard to free people from any understanding of God as a heavenly being who keeps a record of wrongs or who punishes for sin or who would want to inflict suffering on people.

"The constant problem people have with God is what you mentioned a moment ago. People believe everything that happens is in God's hands, under God's control. I don't believe that. When people do believe it, they ask the wrong questions, such as 'Why did God let this or that happen?' or 'When is God going to intervene and help us?' My teaching invites people to anchor their religious faith in the understanding of God's constant presence and inexhaustible love and compassion. Only when they achieve a deep-seated conversion in their thinking about God can they reflect on any painful circumstances in their lives and understand that this is not God's doing. And if God is not responsible, who or what is? And what can we do about it? They are the important questions to be addressed when we experience suffering of any kind rather than trying to work out where God fits into what is happening to us.

But, to return to your question: where does God fit in for me right now? I believe in God's loving presence with me in the midst of all this, despite how strange that may sound to you.

"Let me take this a step further. Since I believe that the Spirit of God is in me, I have to ask, not what a *heavenly* God wants of me, but what the Spirit of God *within* me wants of me. That is like asking what does love, integrity, graciousness, compassion, fidelity, growth, ask of me. This is the challenging question we all must ask and respond to when times become painful and difficult for us.

"There's a choice for us here. Do we choose to look to an overseer God in control of the world and entangle ourselves in distorted notions of God? Or do we choose to call on the presence and the power of God's Spirit with us to help us face the realities of life and to change what we can? Right now, I'm holding onto the presence and power of God's Spirit with me to help me face whatever today brings."

"The Greeks and the Romans tell us our religion is unimportant. They say that only their gods can help us attain immortality, and that's what really matters. What do you think?"

"Since we have co-existed with the Egyptians and the Greeks and the Romans for hundreds of years it's not surprising that we Jews are familiar with their mystery religions. We know their claims about a savior, a man-god person who supposedly established access to the dwelling place of the gods. We've all heard the stories they tell about this savior who had a miraculous birth, who was born in a cave, and who raised people from the dead. He rose from the dead and now holds out the promise of immortality to whoever imbibes his spirit through some kind of ritual meal. This theme is common to the stories we hear about Osiris and Dionysius and Mithras and others. Yes, it's attractive to have a man-god figure who wins immortality for people, but wise people understand that this is all mythology. These man-god persons never really existed. As a Jew, I choose not to base my religious beliefs on these stories."

"But isn't the attainment of immortality an important issue? Don't the mystery religions offer hope to people?"

"I think the issue of immortality is a distraction from the need to establish God's kingdom of justice here, now. I told my apostles not to get sidetracked by the issue of immortality. It is not the important issue. I'm convinced that God's compassion and fidelity will embrace whatever happens in death. I believe this has always been so. We Jews should not be led into believing that it was necessary for a man-god to attain access to God. That belief belongs only to the understanding, such as the Greeks have, that there is no connection between the realm of the gods and life on earth. That thinking is unacceptable to our Jewish belief in God."

"Those other religions are attractive, though. I know some of my friends think seriously about joining them. They don't demand we keep laws the way we Jews are obliged to keep laws, and some of their rituals and festivities look very appealing."

"Even in Galilee we were familiar with the Greek and the Roman religious ideas and practices. Like you here in Jerusalem we couldn't escape their influence and their challenge to our Jewish faith and practices. I have great admiration for the ethical ideals and the concept of human nobility that some of their myths espouse. My own preaching shares much in common with them. On the other hand, the Maccabees didn't see any evidence of the Greeks' noble teaching when the Greeks took over Jerusalem and turned our temple into a Greek temple. They executed anyone who practiced our Jewish religion. Now the Romans rule the world with violence and oppression, and call it 'peace'. For all the talk about human nobility in their religious cults and their concern with gaining immortality, look around and see what sort of society they have created."

"But do you have any interest in or sympathy with the mystery religions?"

"Only in so far as they point to a deep truth about human dignity. If the myths tell us something wonderful about ourselves and challenge us to do great things, fine. But I have no interest or belief in a man-god who gained access to the heavens and now bestows immortality on his followers. And I certainly have no interest in worshipping this person as if he acquired something humans never had. No, we have always had a share in God's life. We have no need of a man-god savior to win that for us. My criticism of the mystery religions is that they focus on the next life and on the man-god figures who win that for us. They downplay the reality of God's presence here on earth. Ultimately, for all their ethical ideals, they demean human existence and the beauty of the world in which we live. I believe religion should focus on *this* life, on God's presence with us *now*, on ourselves giving witness to that presence, and manifesting God's presence on earth.

"If we lived our religion rightly it *would* be attractive. Many people see our laws as a burden, but that's because leadership has lost sight of what the Torah intends. It's there, gifted to us by God, to help us be conscious of God with us in all we do. It exists to remind us that we are God's people and that we are chosen for a privileged task. Our religion ought to be attractive. It should assure everyone that God's Spirit is upon them. Its fruits should be seen in the type of society we create. It's not God's fault if our religion is unattractive. It's our fault and the fault of religious leadership in the community."

"So you would not abolish the Torah in favor of a less restricted way of life?"

"No, I would not. It would make no sense whatever to uproot the heart and soul of our religion. The Torah is not meant to be a burden around our necks. It is meant to help us live in peace, conscious of God's presence in the everyday actions of our lives. That's a blessing, not a burden. I would work instead to help people understand what our religion is really about."

"Yet many people, myself included, find it burdensome to keep all the laws we have."

"That's because the spirit of the law has been strangled by the legal experts, here in Jerusalem and elsewhere. Legal experts! How did we ever allow ourselves to be weighed down by the legal experts and all their petty rulings! I have a simple attitude: respect the law, live conscious of the Spirit of the Lord God within you and other people, and act accordingly. It's very simple. Yet time and time again I've had legal experts complain about me: you cured someone on the Sabbath, you ate this, you did that. They haven't the slightest regard that I might have been helping people or that I am a decent, good-living person. No, they accused me of being *'possessed by Beelzebul'*. I broke some legal ruling that holds their world together and they are fearful that everything will collapse if they permit such behavior. I can only imagine how small-minded their God must be. What's even worse is that they inflict their small-minded, judgmental God on the people. It's not surprising that you and many others find our religion burdensome. That's what I have wanted to change. I believe our religion should and can be liberating, not burdensome."

"But it's not only the legal experts who opposed you?"

"Oh, no. I've had opposition from all quarters. The hardest to deal with came early in my preaching days when my entire family wanted to lock me away. They thought I was insane. Imagine having your own family think you are crazy. That was a very painful time in my life."

"Do they still think you are crazy?"

"Some do, but a few have come to see me in a different light now. I think one of my brothers will carry on my work if anything happens to me."

"Are your parents still alive?"

"My father died shortly before I went to see John at the Jordan River. His death prompted me to set out on my own. My mother is still alive though I haven't seen her for a long time. She thought my father's death had upset my 'sensitive nature', as she called it. When I started to preach she could not understand why I was being so disruptive. I hear from my brother that she is somewhat more understanding these days."

"I'm trying to imagine what you thought you would achieve when you started to preach and tell your stories. Did you imagine you would see any great changes in your lifetime?"

"I did, actually. I had this great dream. I knew I had an encouraging, uplifting message. I knew, too, that it was challenging, but I expected the good news about God's presence among us would underpin a change of attitudes and actions in the people who heard me preach."

"But what were you hoping for? Surely you didn't expect to see a revolution against the temple priesthood or against the Romans?"

"Not exactly a revolution, but a movement in which people came to believe that what I was preaching could set a course for social and religious change in the future. I desperately wanted people to believe what I was telling them about themselves and about God."

"And that dream died?"

"Yes. The dream has died, and I feel brokenhearted about it. I don't know if it was my fault that people never really responded. Could I have approached them in a different way? Should I have taken things more slowly? Should I have stayed longer in some places? I've asked myself many such questions. Or was it because of peoples' life-long attitudes and beliefs that make it impossible for them to embrace a new way of seeing things? I don't really know, but I suspect it's the latter."

"Was there a particular moment when you realized your dream would never be realized?"

"Yes, when I heard of John's death. I can't tell you how numb I felt that day... Maybe 'numb' is not the right word... I felt so many emotions and had so many thoughts racing through my mind. I felt stranded... as if I were in a boat without a sail and I had no energy to row. It seemed as if time stood still. All I wanted to do was go to a quiet place to sit and think and pray. I asked my companions to row me to a secluded place we knew, but people saw me coming and mobbed me when I arrived. I spent some hours with them before getting away on my own. It wasn't until evening that I had the chance to be alone and sort out what I was feeling and thinking. My mind was quite muddled."

"Why should John's death have affected you so deeply? Violence is so commonplace. You must be used to it, surely."

"Yes, that's true, but that particular act of violence was so unexpected. I thought John would be in prison for years. I thought he was safe there. I had always felt a deep connection with him, even though our preaching was different in some ways. We were both trying to change the way things are, in God's name. Herod has no respect for God and human decency. On hearing of John's senseless and brutal death I felt an enormous sense of powerlessness to change anything. I had already realized that I was not getting through to people the way I had dreamed of doing, and I sensed that time was running out for me. I felt tired and alone. And I wondered whether I would be next in line to be murdered."

"If you thought that, why on earth did you come here to Jerusalem and cause such a disturbance? Why didn't you stay in Galilee and continue your preaching and healing where you could be much safer?"

"That's *the* issue I wrestled with in prayer that night. Why continue? Why not just retreat back home? Perhaps I should stop preaching altogether?

"I decided I couldn't back away from everything I had preached. How could I tell people to trust God in tough times, and then retreat when trouble loomed in my own life? If I really believed what I preached, then integrity demanded I stand by my words and demonstrate it.

"I also decided that I would not let my life end the way John's had, dragged off to prison and killed at the whim of a despot. No, I decided I would make a statement with my death. I would stand up and be counted, and people would know I was ready to die for what I believed and preached. So I came to Jerusalem."

"You do have a death wish, after all."

"It's not that I want to die. It's more that integrity has led me to where I now am. That's the important thing."

"And your friends, your apostles, what about them? Will they follow you this far?"

"Oh, no. I imagine that at this moment they have run for cover, every one of them! But someday, yes, I hope they might be as ready as I am to face death for what they believe. But they have a fair way to go yet before that could happen."

"Do you think they will carry on your preaching?"

"I hope so. I can only hope so."

"You don't sound too confident."

"I had a meal with them early this night. As I looked around the room I had a sinking feeling. I thought, my goodness, is this what I am left with? Are these people going to carry on my work? I can tell you, I wasn't filled with confidence."

"How many were there?"

"About twenty, including my apostles and some of the women who have supported us."

"It sounds as though you knew this might be your final meal with them. What did you say to them?"

"Not a great deal. I tried to leave them with images rather than words.

"At the beginning of the meal I shocked them by washing their feet. I wanted them to remember that they are always to be at the service of others. They must never forget that. They must never abuse authority the way religious leaders here in the temple do. They must never see themselves as closer to God or as better than anyone else. If they keep this in mind and are faithful to it I think that my preaching will continue to touch peoples' lives through them. But if they were to ignore it and start lording power and authority over people, they would not be faithful to my preaching and to what I am ready to give my life for."

"You have high expectations. I hope your friends don't let you down."

"I gave them another image that I hope will stay with them and encourage them to spread my message whatever the cost.

"Towards the end of our meal together I made a point of breaking bread slowly and deliberately, saying that this was symbolic of me giving my all for what I believe. Then I asked them to eat the bread to signify their readiness to follow in my footsteps. I invited them to repeat this gesture as a ritual special to them, a special way of remembering me."

"I can imagine that your gesture of breaking the bread and then offering it your friends had a powerful impact on them."

"I hope it did. I desperately want them to remember me and my message and to commit themselves to my way of life. Whenever they eat bread in memory of me I want them to understand that their eating is their way of saying 'Yes' to following my example and my teaching."

"You are asking a lot of your friends. I can understand them and anyone else thinking twice before making such a commitment."

"Perhaps I am, but I'd love to think that my gesture with the bread might become a ritual that will encourage, sustain and challenge them when I am no longer with them. It's quite simple really: break bread in memory of me and eat it as a sign of your commitment to what I gave myself for."

"It seems to me that your gesture of breaking bread was so appropriate. As I look at you here in front of me, beaten and bleeding, bruised and battered the word, 'broken', comes to mind. I don't mean your spirit. That is certainly not broken, and from what I am hearing it's not likely to be. But some people really want you broken. You're paying a high price for what you believe."

"Yes, but I'm not alone in this. You can probably tell stories about members of your own family or among your friends who in the midst of great suffering, when life threatened to break them, that somehow they found an incredible inner strength to endure and not give in to despair."

"Yes, I know people like that. It surprises me no end with some of them. I wonder where they get their incredible courage from."

"Oh, I can answer that for you. They get it from the Spirit of God within them. That's why I say I am not alone in this. I'm not doing something extraordinary. I'm just being true to that Spirit within me, the Spirit that is in everyone. Many people, however, do not see the connection between the Spirit within them and their courageous acts."

"And you keep insisting that the same Spirit is in me."

"Yes. Let's talk about you for a while."

"Oh, no. I'm very ordinary. Don't waste your precious time talking about me. I told you earlier I'm not anyone special."

"See, that's where you and so many other people go wrong. 'Oh, no, not me, the Spirit of God cannot really be in me.' The Egyptians do it, the Greeks do it, the Romans do it, and we Jews do it! Oh, no, say the Greeks and the Romans, let us have a man-god figure who really has the spirit of the gods in him in a special way. Then we can all gather round and worship him and get some glimmer of hope for immortality, all the while carrying the belief that we are nothing like this amazing man-god. And we Jews, rather than using the Torah to be conscious of God with us in our everyday lives, we turn it into a burden imposed on a God-forsaken people. When will this ever stop?! I urge you to start reflecting on your everyday experience of being a decent and caring man. Recognize and name the goodness you see in yourself as the movement of God's Spirit in you. The Spirit is there. It's just that you fail to see the connection between your basic goodness and the Spirit of God in you. It's simple really."

"Or maybe you are just being simplistic and misguided."

"Try doing it for yourself and then decide whether I am misguided or not. But you have to try it. I believe you'll be surprised and delighted by what you find. Just reflect on your good actions and start to connect and identify those actions with the presence of God's Spirit in you. Will you do that whenever you recall this night? Will you help your family to do it also?"

"I will consider doing so. I can't promise you more than that… But let me ask you another question, and this will probably have to be my last one since morning is upon us. With all your talk about changing society and establishing the kingdom of God, do you think you are God's promised Messiah?"

"No, no, no. When I spoke earlier about believing I was anointed by God, it had nothing to do with the way many Jewish people expect God to raise up a great Anointed One to re-establish the Kingdom of Israel. I've tried to make that clear to my apostles and my followers. That is not who I am. I'm simply the human face of God's Spirit. I am no different from you or anyone else in that. We're all called to be the human face of God in the world. My dream about the kingdom of God includes everyone and challenges everyone to participate. I want nothing to do with a political, religious institution that would set itself up as uniquely belonging to God."

"I must ask one more question, then. What of Judaism? What is our future as God's chosen people?"

"There is no one way for people to honor God. There is only one great commandment that everyone should embrace. All Jews know it. Judaism must be a light to the world. It must attract people by its God-consciousness, by its care for everyone and by its concern for justice. However, Judaism, like any other religion, must grow beyond exclusive claims of intimacy with or knowledge of God. The Spirit of God is everywhere and cannot be contained within one group, sect or religion. The Spirit is evident in everyone who loves and cares and tries to be neighbor. All religions should espouse this belief and use it to challenge their followers to embody this Spirit in the way they treat others. Religions must respect everyone as a child of God."

"I must go now. I hear movement upstairs and I mustn't be found in here with you. Before I go, let me say one final thing. People call me Tim, but my full name is Timaeus. Although I work here in Jerusalem, my wife and family live in Jericho. When you were there a week ago you met my blind son, Bartimaeus, on the roadside. He had called out to you and you stopped and spoke with him. You then cured his blindness. I've wanted to find you and thank you and get to know you. I was deeply shocked to arrive here and find it was you in this dreadful condition. Now I may never see you again. I'm so sorry for what is happening to you here. But I want you to know that my family and I will never, never forget you."

"Thank you, Tim. And please, don't just remember your son's cure. Please remember my teaching that goes with it. Please do that."

"We will. I promise you. Shalom, my friend."

"Shalom, my friend."

PART 2

Historical Background

Alexander the Great (356 – 323 BC) established the Greek empire which incorporated Palestine 330 years before Jesus was born.

In 174 BC, Jason, the High Priest in Jerusalem, co-operated with the Greek ruler, Antiochus Epiphanes, to turn Jerusalem into a Greek city.

In 167 BC, Antiochus outlawed Judaism and renamed the temple as "The Temple of the Olympian Zeus". Antiochus ordered the execution of anyone who did not adopt Greek customs.

The Maccabean revolt against Greek control over the temple and the suppression of Judaism succeeded in 164 BC. However, Greek rule over Palestine continued.

In 63 BC, Palestine came under the control of the Roman Empire.

Jesus, like most Jews of his day, would have been familiar with Greek and Roman culture. For three hundred years before the time of Jesus, Greek was the language of government and business in Palestine. Anyone who travelled, even in Galilee, would have been exposed to the influence of Greek culture, language and architecture.

Judaism had to confront the attraction of Greek and Roman culture and their religious cults, the 'mystery' religions. These cults focused on myths with variations about a man-god, a 'Son of God' who had 'saved the world' by conquering the forces of evil, had gained access to the heavenly dwelling place of the gods, and could thereby bestow immortality on people who participated in the cults.

In response to Greek and Roman rule, the Pharisees advocated stronger fidelity to the Torah. The Essenes withdrew from society altogether. The Zealots waged resistance. The Sadducees and business leaders, along with Herod the Great and his sons, unashamedly committed themselves to conformity with Greek and Roman culture and influence.

Jesus did not address the premises, worldviews or myths of the Greek-Roman mystery religions. He showed no interest in religious thinking that separated God from involvement with daily life on earth.

Jesus died a faithful Jew. He did not renounce his Judaism. He did not start a new religion. He did not ordain anyone. He did not establish a new cultic priesthood.

St. Peter and all the apostles and St. Paul, who died more than thirty years after Jesus, died as Jews. Peter was never the head of a new religion separate from Judaism. 'Peter the first Pope' is myth, not fact.

The Christian religion did not become an entity separate from Judaism until at least fifty years after Jesus died. It did not begin at the Jewish feast of Pentecost in the year Jesus died.

Mark's gospel, the first gospel, was written around 70 AD, about the time Jerusalem and the temple were destroyed by the Romans. There is no infancy account, and in the earliest edition of the gospel there are no resurrection stories of Jesus appearing to people.

St. Paul took the message of Jesus not only to the Gentiles who had some connection with Judaism, but also to the Greek-Roman world. As he engaged the Greek-Roman world, Paul faced the challenge of showing that Jesus was more important and more influential than any of the man-god saviors of the mystery religions.

Matthew's gospel reveals the tension within a Jewish community in the 80's. On the one hand, the author presents Jesus and his message as faithful to Judaism: *"Don't even begin to think that I have come to do away with the Law and the Prophets. I haven't come to do away with them but to fulfil them… Whoever ignores one of the least of these commands and teaches others to do the same will be called the lowest in the kingdom of heaven."* (5:17-19) On the other hand, there is the historical reality, which is hinted at in chapter 24 of Matthew's gospel, of strife in the community leading to the expulsion of the followers of Jesus from the community. The leaders of the Jewish community would have been disturbed, not by Jesus' message, carefully presented in the gospel as faithful to Judaism, but by the claims made by some Jews about the Christ figure which undermined the importance of the Law and presented Jesus as a man-god savior of the world.

Expulsion from Jewish communities eventually led to the establishment of a new religion separate from Judaism. This religion based its identity on the understanding that only through membership of this new religion and belief in its Christ could people attain everlasting life with God in heaven.

PART 3

Remembering Jesus. 75 AD

"Shalom, Bartimaeus. My name is Ezra. Would you have some time to talk with me? I have made a long journey to see you."

"Shalom, Ezra. Really? You have come a long way to talk with an old man? I am honored. Please come in and make yourself comfortable."

"Thank you. Let me tell you about myself and you will understand why I wish to talk with you.

"I lived in Jerusalem until ten years ago when I heard the Romans were planning to attack the city. I moved to a distant place called Hierapolis, most of which had been destroyed by an earthquake five years earlier. I'd heard there was a great need for skilled workers to begin rebuilding the city, so I went there with quite a number of other Jewish workers. Our Jewish presence has grown considerably in the past few years. Even though our living conditions are not ideal, we can see that this city has a future and will one day become important again. However, we are now experiencing divisions among ourselves, and the divisions are becoming hurtful and painful. People are taking sides, not talking to one another, and calling one another bad names. We hear that we are not alone in this and that the same thing is happening in other Jewish communities also."

"Yes. It happens here, too, and I fear it will become worse. But why have you come to talk with me about this?"

"First, let me say that I have not made this journey on my own initiative. I come on behalf of my friends. Your encounter as a young man with Jesus is well-known, especially now that it has been recorded in writing. What a wonderful gift it must have been to have had your sight restored! When we heard you were still alive and that you have been an integral part of the Way of Jesus since his death, we decided to seek your advice. We urgently need some direction because of the turmoil in which we find ourselves. The apostles are all dead. Paul is dead. Jerusalem and the temple have been destroyed. Our people have been dispersed, and, as if all that is not bad enough, we find ourselves in bitter dispute with one another about how to follow the Way of Jesus and still remain faithful to our religion. Some of my friends and I are newcomers to the Way of Jesus. I knew very little about it when I lived in Jerusalem. We think it's important that we believe and follow what Jesus wanted us to believe and follow, but that is not as easy to do as we would like. There are conflicting opinions about Jesus in our midst. We want to know which are most faithful to Jesus and his message."

"Let me offer you something to drink and eat, and then you can tell me about the divisions in your community."

. . .

"Now, what is happening in this faraway city of yours?"

"We find ourselves divided into three groups. There are those who have no interest whatever in Jesus and his Way. They are supported and encouraged by our synagogue leaders who are trying desperately to keep our Jewish community faithful to the Torah. They are convinced the temple was destroyed as God's punishment for our lack of fidelity to the Covenant and they are deeply disturbed by the beliefs and attitudes of the second group. Members of this group promote and discuss the letters of Paul. They consider Paul to be the most authoritative voice on understanding Jesus. They call Jesus, 'Christ', as if that were his real name. They make claims and tell stories about this Christ figure which are clearly borrowed from the Greek and Roman religions, yet are made to sound as if they were historical facts about Jesus."

"Yes. I have heard the stories. His mother was a virgin impregnated by God; he was born in a cave with shepherds and Magi paying their respects; he turned water into wine; he raised people from the dead; he was the good shepherd; he was the Son of God; he died for the sins of the world; he conquered death; he rose after three days; he went to heaven; he has made immortality possible for all of us, and he will be the judge of everyone at the end times. It's quite a list!

"What puzzles me is that we Jews know the origin of these stories. We know they come from the pagan cults. We know they are myth, not fact. It not only puzzles me, but deeply troubles me to hear followers of Jesus applying these stories to Jesus when we know they are not factual details of his life."

"That is precisely what disturbs those of us in the third group. Not too many years after Jesus died some of our group heard Peter and James speak about Jesus. They say there was no mention of these things then. We believe these stories about Jesus are not true. They are false embellishments on his life. However, the stories continue to be spread, creating confusion about how we are to understand Jesus. Without these stories, we believe most of our community would have few problems accepting and living the Way of Jesus. We would dearly love to talk to Peter or James or any of Jesus' apostles about what is happening, but since that is not possible, someone suggested I find you. You are one of the few people alive today who met Jesus. You are our only link to him and to the beginnings of his Way within Judaism."

"You remind me of how old I am! Yes, the joy of my life is not only to have my sight, but to have met Jesus and to have spent my life keeping his memory and his dream alive.

"I should add that my father also had a profound influence on me. After Jesus healed me of my blindness, I decided to follow him. I was living here in Jericho at the time. When I heard that Jesus was on his way to Jerusalem, I decided I would go there and become one of his disciples. I had barely got over the celebrations here in Jericho that I was able to see when we heard the news that Jesus had been crucified. I thought that was the end of that. Then, shortly afterwards, my father came to see me and told me the most remarkable story: he was on guard duty the night before Jesus' execution. What made it even more extraordinary was that he had spent the night in conversation with Jesus rather than merely guarding him. Afterwards, my father was insistent that all of his family, and I especially, had to keep the memory of Jesus alive. He kept saying that the healing of my blindness must not be separated from the message that Jesus preached. We must faithfully remember and hand on Jesus' *message*, not just the story of the healing. I have been blessed with an unusually long life and I have tried to be faithful in handing on that message, so maybe my experience may be of help to you."

"I hope so. I have so many questions! Tell me, did you ever hear Paul speak?"

"Yes. Several times. He was quite an orator, very intense and passionate about what he believed. I was struck by how different he was from Jesus. Jesus was... How can I describe it?... Gentler, more quietly persuasive, not at all intimidating. There was something about Jesus that spoke volumes. There was something commanding, appealing, without the need for many words. Many people related how he spoke with the authority of personal experience. He spoke simply. He never lectured people and he had a wonderful way of touching the ordinary, everyday experiences of peoples' lives. And another thing, when I was close to Jesus I sensed a strong inner power or presence that seemed to reach out and embrace me. I know other people had the same experience. I have heard many people speak about him in this way.

"With Paul it was different. It was Paul presenting his grand vision. He didn't seem interested in the person of Jesus, the man we had known. He gave no time to Jesus' teaching. He was more interested in 'the Christ' and how this Christ figure was part of God's plan to set everything right with God again."

"Why do you think Paul didn't focus on Jesus' message?"

"I think it was a great pity that Paul never met Jesus. It showed in his speeches and it shows in his letters that he did not know Jesus personally. There is no doubt Paul had a powerful visionary experience of Jesus and it changed the course of his life. But in not meeting the Jesus we knew I think Paul allowed his mystical experience to become his authority. That experience set him on the path of spreading his own larger-than-life ideas about God, the Law, salvation and the Christ rather than focusing on what Jesus had actually preached.

"As I mentioned, my father kept insisting: keep the message of Jesus alive. Paul did that to some extent, but not faithfully enough. He spoke about the Way and how radical it was in practice. He spoke about equality and love and mercy. Yes, he did that, but when I heard him speak, his primary concern was the Christ figure who he believed had ushered in a new era of salvation and access to God. I came away thinking Paul had taken his eyes and his mind off Jesus and Jesus' focus on establishing the kingdom of God here and now."

"Was there anything else you noticed about Paul's preaching?"

"In the years that followed Jesus' death, we followers of the Way focused on how Jesus lived what he preached.

Telling the stories about him sustained and encouraged us. The more we told the stories, the more we gained insight about his message and the more our appreciation deepened that God's power and presence were at work in him. I cannot stress how important that was for us. The more we gathered in his name and told the stories, the more his message deepened within and among us. I think the stories helped us become the fertile ground he referred to in some of his stories. As the months and years went by, we became convinced that the same power and presence that were in Jesus were in each of us. The stories changed us. They were not just stories about Jesus. They were stories telling us that God's power and presence are within each of us, just as they were within Jesus.

"But, with Paul it was different. Although he preached and wrote that we are all temples of God's Spirit, Paul was an ideas man. He preached great ideas. I'm not saying they were wrong. Some were definitely in accord with Jesus' message. But I think he got carried away with his ideas. His visionary ideas about the struggle between heaven and earth took him along a different path from the one Jesus walked and preached. Paul became obsessed, I think, with the idea that Jesus won forgiveness from God and that he had achieved immortality for us."

"You don't think Jesus was concerned with those issues?"

"What I know is that these notions were never our concern when we gathered and told our stories about Jesus. People who had heard Jesus speak were fond of recalling that he referred to them as *children of God*. Jesus would say that when people are compassionate and worked for justice they would *see* God or would know God is with them. We all experienced that. We had a strong sense of a family relationship with God. We viewed God as a loving parent. We believed we were the loved sons and daughters of God. This is not new to us Jews, but Jesus emphasized it strongly. He was very clear about it: it is through their care and concern for others that people would come to know deep down their intimate connection with God.

"But when I heard Paul preach or when I hear about some of the things he has written, I've noticed a different approach altogether. He emphasized sin and that humanity was at odds with God. One of his phrases is embedded in my mind: we were all *'dead in our sins'*. According to Paul, his Christ won God's forgiveness and rescued us from a world cloaked in sinfulness. Paul taught that only through Christ achieving this could any one of us become a 'child' of God. Paul's Christ *won* that status for us. That's not what Jesus believed or taught. He did not consider himself as someone who won God's friendship with us. He took for granted that God's presence has always been with us and that we had to believe this good news. He did not win it for us. He would never have claimed or believed anything like that. He wanted us to experience God with us as he experienced God with him. It would have been inconceivable to Jesus to think that God's presence only came to people through an intermediary or that an intermediary would have to *win* God's forgiveness.

"I firmly believe that Jesus would reject any notion that God withheld forgiveness. That was not his idea of God. Anyone who teaches that God forgave humanity only because of something Jesus did would be implying that Jesus was wrong in his thinking and teaching about God. There's the choice to be made: Do we accept Jesus' teaching about God being a gracious presence always with us or do we follow other ideas about a distant God who withdrew and withheld forgiveness?"

"Something else that troubles many of us is the suggestion that the Torah has been superseded. Have you heard talk of this?"

"Yes, I have heard that, too. I once heard Paul speak about the Torah. He went on at length about living under the Law and freedom from the Law. He said that only through the Spirit of God being released when Jesus was taken up into heaven could we be set free and be adopted as God's children. He believed the Torah could never set us free. Like people in your community I found it all very disturbing because it had nothing to do with anything Jesus said. I think Jesus would honor the Torah as a way of living God-consciously in our everyday living as long as we live its spirit and not turn it into legalism. I've heard many people quote Jesus' assertion that nothing should ever be erased from the Law, and that anyone who ignored the Law should be called the lowest in God's kingdom. That's quite a challenge for people who follow Paul's teaching and who maintain that following the Christ gives them the right, even the duty, to set the Law aside."

"I am pleased to hear you say that. We do not want to abandon our time-honored adherence to the Law."

"And respecting the Law does not interfere with or contradict Jesus' message that the Spirit of God is with us in all we do."

"What about the resurrection of Jesus? We are now hearing new stories about Jesus appearing to people after he died and then going up to heaven. Do you know what really happened?"

"Yes. I have heard these new stories and they keep appearing in ways that astonish me. Well, maybe I should not be astonished since I have some understanding of why the stories emerged and where they come from.

"When Jesus was executed, panic set in among his closest companions. Most of them fled from Jerusalem. When I came to Jerusalem several weeks after Jesus died not one of the apostles was there. I had difficulty making contact with his followers in Jerusalem because they met in secrecy, and they were all very afraid and quite disillusioned. There was no dramatic raising of Jesus from death three days after he died. It was nothing like that, but what happened was every bit as miraculous, and it led to the same conclusion: God had raised Jesus from death.

"Initially we struggled with many questions. How could God abandon this man who loved God so greatly? Could we not trust God to reward someone who put his trust in God's goodness? Is this the end, and this man's life and preaching come to nothing? Is this what God wants? Does evil prevail and we are to live without hope?"

"Oh, yes, we were lost and disillusioned for some weeks and months. Then the miracle happened. At least I consider it a miracle granted the state of mind we were in, and how so many of us were changed in mind and attitude in a short time. I think everything changed for us when we realized we were asking the same questions that were raised when the Maccabees and their followers were executed or killed in battle. Like them we were tormented and wondering where God could be in this time of pain and disillusionment. We looked for comfort and guidance from one another and from our scriptures. It was the words of the prophet Hosea that helped to break us from our anxiety and darkness. I'm sure you know the passage where he urged people to return to the Lord so that he may heal and bind them up after suffering. And then, those wonderful words, *'After two days he will revive us, and on the third day he will raise us up so that we may live before him... His coming is as sure as the dawn; he will come to us like the spring rains that water the earth.'*

"Finally, awareness dawned for us. Yes, God can be trusted to raise up and give new life to the Maccabees, and to Jesus! The Spirit of the Lord finally broke through within and among us with the conviction, 'Of course!! Of course, God would not leave his faithful friends who had died among the lifeless in sheol. Of course, God would 'awaken' them and 'raise' them to new life with him. Of course, Jesus has been raised by God! Death is not the end! Evil has not triumphed! Jesus lives on!'

"Maybe you can imagine how this awareness changed everything for us and gave us courage and hope and a new understanding of life and death and our relationship with God. We went from being scared and huddling together to being men and women who knew that the Spirit of the Lord we had seen in Jesus was more powerful than the power of death - and that it was now breaking through to the surface in our lives as it had in Jesus. That was some miracle, believe me! In the words of Hosea, God had 'revived' us as well!

"We did not take the "third day" literally. In Hosea it is symbolic language, bearing the conviction that God will act. We now believed God had acted in raising Jesus from sheol. The story about Jesus being raised literally three days after he died took years to develop.

"The stories about an empty tomb and Jesus ascending into the heavens appeared much later, and we know they were copied from the Greek and Roman stories about their man-god figures who rose from the dead and won immortality for us. That's what is disturbing about them: they link Jesus' death with winning immortality for us, and that's not what we ever believed. Our focus was on God vindicating Jesus and his message by raising him from among the dead."

"What about the older stories we have heard, that Jesus appeared to people after he died? Are they not true? Paul certainly thought they were. You must have heard those stories or witnessed what actually happened."

"People certainly experienced Jesus appearing to them. That definitely happened, over and over. It's interesting. I've always felt very close to Jesus, yet he never appeared to me! However, I have been privileged to hear people speak of their encounters with him and I believe they were real. But you have to understand that those encounters were mostly through dreams and visions that followed intense periods of prayer and sharing. The encounters always seemed to deepen the awareness of the men and women who had them that in some mysterious way Jesus remained close to them even in death. These experiences had nothing to do with Jesus ascending into heaven and winning God's forgiveness for us and making us children of God."

"Did Jesus say anything about life after death? How did the early followers of the Way think about it?"

"What I have always appreciated and enjoyed in knowing and hearing people who knew Jesus better than I, was hearing again and again the simple stories Jesus told about important issues. At the heart of these stories was Jesus' conviction that God is gracious beyond all measure. And of course we tell these stories now in the light of our belief in God's graciousness in raising Jesus from the dead. I'm sure you know some of the stories: the wayward son returning home to his father, or the vineyard owner who is generous to all his workers. I like the one about the sheep and goats. We have enjoyed that story so much. We are all sheep! Not one of us is a goat! So let us rejoice in God's presence now and be assured of entering into God's presence when we die. It's truly wonderful to know we are sheep!

"See, that's the wonder of Jesus' teaching. It's so simple, yet so powerful. It turns the way we think about ourselves upside down. It is a message that encourages and empowers us as we think of ourselves in relation with this wonderful God of ours.

"As we keep telling the stories and keep thinking about them, we better understand the message behind the stories: God is indeed gracious; we are richly blessed; we are set free from fear of God, free from any fear of what might happen beyond death. When we have come to know God's loving presence with us in life we come to trust that this loving presence will remain with us when we die.

"To answer your question: I think Jesus took for granted that whatever lies beyond death is in the hands of God, gracious and loving beyond anything we can imagine. We are not to worry about it."

"If Jesus' teaching was so simple and clear, why are we hearing teachings that he never mentioned?"

"It's clear that Paul and others attempted to bring our Jewish faith to the Greeks and the Romans. I commend them for that. As a loyal Jew till the day he died, Paul was not intentionally trying to undermine our religion. He was trying to expand our Jewish influence and prestige by engaging the most topical religious question of the pagan religions, the issue of immortality. He might have been better advised to emphasize what we Jews have always believed, that God is personally interested in us, is engaged in our affairs, is compassionate and merciful and can be trusted to reward those who are faithful to Him. As you know, the idea of a God who is personally interested in events on earth bewilders the Greeks and Romans. It is foreign to their worldview. For the Greeks, there can be no connection between the changeless perfection of heaven and this material, changing, imperfect world. But once you engage that worldview, as Paul did, you have to interpret Jesus in it. He had to demonstrate that Jesus could and did bridge the void between heaven and earth. He had to make Jesus not only equal to but of much higher importance than the mythical pagan man-gods who gained access to heaven. Without such a claim, Jesus would have no relevance for Greek and Roman religious thinkers.

"A problem we have now is that educated pagans know some followers of Jesus are using pagan ideas and myths to present Jesus to the world. They know their myths are not factual stories about people who actually lived. Already some of them are laughing at the followers of Jesus who have borrowed their stories about the offspring of a god and a virgin, about someone born in a cave as shepherds rejoiced, about someone who miraculously rose from death three days after he died, and presenting them as facts about Jesus. It is a shame to see these educated people holding followers of Jesus up for ridicule. We don't need or want this to be happening.

"I met Jesus and I became friends with many people who knew him well. The Jesus we knew was very human, like the rest of us. His mother certainly knew nothing about a miraculous conception. Jesus never gave the impression that he was different from or superior to anyone else. He constantly referred to himself as '*the human one*'. Never did his belief and faith in the Spirit of God moving in him set him above the people he mixed with every day. What constantly impressed people about Jesus was that he never talked down to them. He spoke rather with the authority of someone who knew the everyday struggles of life."

"Someone in our community recently quoted Paul's claims that '*Everyone in heaven, on earth, and under the earth should bow and confess that Jesus is Lord*' and that '*All things exist through him and we live through him.*' Surely that is going too far!"

"I share your concern. I fear that if these ideas persist, the real Jesus will become unrecognizable. He will be overshadowed by the Christ created from the pagan myths. What a tragedy that would be. This is not the Jesus who conversed with my father the night before he died. This is not how Jesus wanted to be remembered.

"We must make sure that he is not turned into a man-god or give him attributes that rightly belong to God alone. We must not be distracted by grand ideas that would turn our attention away from the Way of Jesus and its focus on establishing God's kingdom of justice and mercy on earth.

"But now, let us rest awhile, and talk more a little later. You must surely be weary from your journey."

...

"Now that you have rested, what else concerns you about following the Way of Jesus?"

"I want to ask you about our custom of breaking and sharing bread when we meet and how the ritual was understood in the earliest days. We are becoming more and more confused by language that suggests the bread is '*the body*' of Jesus. Do you know where this confusion came from?"

"In one of the Roman mystery religions that honors him, Mithras is claimed to have said, 'Whoever does not eat my body and drink my blood, so that he will become one with me and I with him, cannot know salvation.' The followers of Mithras believe that when they gather and eat in memory of him they take his life-giving and immortal spirit into themselves. However, they do not take literally his words about eating his body. They do not believe they eat the actual body or drink the blood of Mithras. The words and actions are full of mysterious meanings that only his followers can appreciate. That's the point of these mystery religions: the words and actions are symbolic of great mystery that the participants find uplifting, ennobling and hopeful.

"When we started to gather in our homes in memory of Jesus, some members of our group were familiar with those words of Mithras, even though none of us participated in that Roman cult. Despite their pagan origin, the words rang true for us. In some mysterious way, when we shared the bread and the wine in memory of Jesus, we experienced closeness to him and the Spirit that was upon him. We sensed a wonderful connection with him. But we never focused on *what* we were eating, the bread itself. We certainly did not identify the bread with the physical body of Jesus. No, never. It was the *action* of eating that was important because it symbolized our determination to follow Jesus as he had asked of us.

"The word, 'body', can be very confusing. This is one time when we could take a lead from the pagans. We should appreciate the symbolism and mystery conveyed when we use 'body', 'flesh' and 'blood' in our rituals commemorating Jesus. We must be careful not to understand those words in a literal sense."

"That's very helpful. I know I have been confused by 'body' language. I like the way you linked it with the pagans' sense of mystery. It really is spiritual, symbolic language when we repeat Jesus' words, '*This is my body*'. I see the parallel with saying that we are 'the body of Christ'. This is also spiritual, mystical language, isn't it?"

"Although I have reservations about how the word 'Christ' is used, I hope that understanding '*the body of Christ*' symbolically might help people appreciate being bonded with Jesus, being in union with him, being of the same mind as he, being willing to manifest the same Spirit he did, and being bonded with one another as a body of believers."

"I am relieved to hear what you have just shared. To be *'the body of Christ'* is both affirming and challenging. And I must say I like the way Paul has written about that, urging his readers to act as one body, not as divided groups. Unfortunately, his followers seem to believe that thinking and acting as one body means thinking and acting in accordance with their beliefs, so in practice we followers of Jesus are divided and are not acting as one body.

"Our synagogue leaders are increasingly frustrated by the divisions in our community, so those of us who follow the Way are under pressure from two sides, our leaders and the followers of Paul. If we cannot resolve our differences, I would not be surprised if we were expelled from the community."

"I doubt that you would be expelled simply for following Jesus. It would be far more likely to happen because these new stories about him are unacceptable to our religion. Judaism cannot be expected to tolerate belief in Jesus as a man-god figure who undermines the importance of the Torah."

"Yes, but I fear that our synagogue leaders will not distinguish between those of us who follow Paul's ideas and those who want to stay loyal to the Way of Jesus. I fear a total spilt between our religion and anyone who professes any kind of faith in Jesus.

"Do you think it would be possible for the followers of Jesus to unite around his message and allow other differences to be secondary to this? Could we not, in the name of Jesus, accept our differences?"

"I do not want to be a pessimist, but I foresee, as you yourself fear, in the not too distant future a major split between Jews who accept Jesus and Jews who do not accept him. When that happens, I'm convinced there will be a further split among the followers of Jesus because I doubt that their differences in thinking can be reconciled. From what you have told me, the three groups in your community will each go their separate ways and the parting will be very painful, especially for your group. You will be isolated and ostracized. But I do not think your community is unique in all this. I fear the synagogue leaders here and in other places are equally alarmed by what is happening in their communities."

"Tell me more. What do see happening?"

"I have spoken with wiser people than I about this. There is general agreement that the expelled followers of Jesus will either become a cult within Judaism, or, unfortunately, they will cut themselves off from Judaism and form a new religion altogether. If they were to separate, they would need to adopt an identity quite distinct from Judaism to promote their new religion."

"If we were expelled, it would be a big concern for my friends and me if Paul's ideas came to dominate and give identity to the breakaway group."

"Regrettably, I believe that is inevitable if that group continues to engage the pagan world and its religious mythologies."

"Do you think our group will be cast aside by this new movement if we continue to resist its thinking about the Christ?"

"I wish your group and others like it could stay within Judaism and honor Jesus as a great prophetical figure and promote his way of life. But I do think the future will bring a total break of all followers of Jesus from our cherished religion. That is so sad and painful to contemplate, but I and others see it as the most likely outcome of the divisions among us. Believers like us will be expelled, not because we follow Jesus, but because people have made Jesus into an unacceptable man-god before whom everyone must kneel and bow and confess as 'Lord'. These people will inevitably claim, as Paul has, that only through faith in the Christ figure can anyone attain a place in heaven. We, in turn, will not be considered loyal enough to this movement and its claims about exclusive access to God. I think it will turn against us as well in order to protect its teachings about the Christ."

"That is an unhappy prospect. It is not what I came here to hear. I will return home not knowing what to do!"

"Nothing has changed. You came here committed to Jesus and his message. I hope you will leave here with the same, or an even a deeper, commitment. Whatever the future holds, there will be people who want to remain faithful to the Jesus who walked and talked with us. They will promote his message as good news, as the way to set people free, as the way to ennoble them and to challenge them to let God's Spirit shine in their lives. Like me, you are part of that movement.

"When I first became a follower of Jesus I understood that his Way of living was my salvation. I experienced that. I was set free from fear of God, from anxiety about death, from dependence on superstition and from scruples about keeping the Law. The community gatherings helped me become aware that the Spirit of the Lord is upon me as it was upon Jesus. I gained a wonderful appreciation that everyone around me carried the same Spirit. None of that should change if we are faithful in handing on Jesus' message. We will need to be steadfast in resisting the idea that salvation is about getting into heaven as if Jesus accomplished something totally new and only he could accomplish it."

"What do you foresee for Judaism in the midst of all this?"

"I see difficult times ahead for Judaism as well, now that Jerusalem and the temple have been destroyed. Our dream of Jerusalem being a light to the nations is in ruins. I saw the message of Jesus as a sign of hope for Judaism. It is a prophetic message, not really new to us. We have always been taught that we are not to be proud-hearted, that we are to work for peace and justice, that we are to be merciful, that we are to abhor violence, and that we are to create families and societies that highlight God's presence with us. Jesus' message resonates with the heart and soul of our religion. His focus on God's presence with us is a powerful encouragement for us to be faithful to our true identity as Jews.

"And now, if Judaism rejects the message of Jesus I fear it will face many years in the wilderness. It presently lacks the prophetical leadership that Jesus demonstrated."

"The future looks grim for both our religion and our group. What, then, of this movement that gathers around Paul's thinking? Do you think it will last, or will it just die out?"

"I sincerely hope it does not last. What worries me most about it, apart from being a distraction from what Jesus really died for, is that it is elitist. Think about this: Judaism could never become the religion of the Roman Empire. Oh, yes, our temple establishment did all it could to work with both the Greek and Roman rulers for financial gain, but Judaism has always been seen as an oddity by our foreign rulers. But this new movement is adapting itself to Greek and Romans ideas, borrowing their religious stories and shaping its understanding of Christ in accord with their notions of a man-god who wins access to the heavens. Its adherents are already proclaiming that only through having the Spirit of the Christ can anyone get to heaven and that only the Christ bestows God's Spirit on humans. In direct opposition to Jesus' preaching, clear instructions and warnings, this movement has the potential of aligning itself to imperial power by the way it preaches the all-conquering Christ."

"I hear your concerns, but on the other hand, should we not give some credit to the followers of Paul? They call for a new world order quite different from what we have now. They look for and work for peace, justice, and care of the poor. They profess and live a radical equality for all people. They say Jesus offers peace in a way the Romans cannot deliver. Their ecclesia movement is a call to live differently. Is not all that positive and hopeful?"

"Indeed it is, but you can have all that without Jesus being presented as the Jewish equivalent of Mithras or Dionysius or any of those other semi-god figures. We, who remember Jesus and seek to keep his memory alive, do not accept any such ideas. They only lead to confusion and trouble."

"What do you suggest I take back home to my friends in Hierapolis?"

"Urge them to live, as Jesus did, the very best ideals of our Jewish faith. Urge them to trust that the Spirit of the Lord is upon them. Urge them to be inclusive as Jesus was. Urge them to resist the claims of Paul's followers about the Christ being necessary for salvation. Urge them to remember Jesus, 'the human one', the person people saw and heard and touched. This is so important. He was not a mythical being. He was real. Keep his reality and his message alive. Urge your friends to be steadfast in the face of opposition and even persecution.

"And tell them that this old man, so wonderfully touched by the hands of Jesus, is deeply bonded with them and believes they are following the right path."

"Thank you, Bartimaeus, for your time and your wise words. Whatever the future holds for us and those who follow the Way of Jesus as we do, I hope your advice will help us to stay close to Jesus and remain loyal to his message."

"I sit here quietly day after day and I think about my life and about Jesus. I think about how we have tried to stay faithful to him. I think about the future and what it holds. I wonder how people will remember Jesus in the years to come. Will they know, really know, the Jesus I knew and love so greatly?

"Please keep his memory alive the way he wanted to be remembered."

PART 4

My Story
1941 - 1992

Like any Catholic boy educated in a Catholic school in the 1940s and 1950s, I knew all about Jesus Christ at an early age. By the time I finished elementary school, the 'certain knowledge' of Catholic faith had been deeply planted in my mind. I learned, and believed unquestioningly, that Jesus had been virginally conceived, that his mother knew he was God incarnate, that he knew he had pre-existed in heaven, that he talked regularly with God his heavenly Father, that he had walked on water, that he founded the only true Church the night before he died, that he had died for my sins, that by dying on the cross he had opened the 'gates of heaven' for us, that he physically ascended into heaven, that he had sent the Spirit of God down to earth at Pentecost, and that baptism into his Church, the Catholic Church, saved us from hell.

I took this knowledge about Jesus Christ into and throughout my teenage years in a pre- Vatican II Church, an era of intense loyalty to the Pope, to Rome, to pride in being Catholic.

I also took this knowledge into my novitiate training as a Missionary of the Sacred Heart (MSC) in 1961. When I was ordained in May, 1969, my thinking about Jesus was that of the theology text books. It would never have occurred to me to question the Christology we were taught. I continued to believe that Jesus knew he had been sent from his Father in heaven. I had learned more about the Catholic Church's 'mystery of religion' which proclaimed that Jesus had two natures, a divine nature and a human nature, while everyone else had only a human nature. I heard more about the beatific vision which granted Jesus immediate communication with God the Father. I wrestled, as most theology students do, with the doctrine that Jesus had, alongside his human will and human knowledge, a divine will and divine knowledge. I understood this to mean that Jesus always knew what God's eternal plan for saving humanity entailed and always knew what was ahead for him. He certainly knew he had been sent to die on the cross for our sins. I understood from Church teaching that in the person of Jesus the Divine will was always in control of his human will and his emotions.

I knew a lot about Jesus Christ, and I firmly believed it all. With ordination I received the Church's official approval that I had the necessary theological knowledge to take the Church's teaching about God, Jesus Christ, the Church and the Sacraments to the world.

It took many years before I became sufficiently aware to articulate the fundamental problem with my lengthy and rigorous education into the Catholic faith. I knew a lot *about* Jesus Christ. I could preach about Jesus Christ. I could teach the Church's theology about Jesus Christ. But I did not know Jesus personally.

What follows here is the story of how I came to *know* Jesus and how I have come to think he should be remembered.

Shortly after ordination I read a book authored by the renowned Catholic scripture scholar, Raymond Brown, in which he raised the questions: What if Jesus, while still being the Son of God, did not comprehend in his humanity who he really was? What if Jesus hanging on the cross did not know he was God incarnate?

Those questions made me stop and think in a way I never had. The fact they had been raised by a Catholic scripture scholar was an invitation to expand my thinking about Jesus in a new light.

For the first time in my life I began to think of Jesus dying on the cross in terms of a faith experience. What an act of faith it must have been if Jesus in his humanity did not know who he really was. I was being invited now to consider and to personally engage a Jesus I had never known. As I thought about this, I did not call into question the traditional understanding of Jesus' divinity. I tried to balance what the Church taught about Jesus having a fully divine nature, while I seriously considered the *human* reality, the human nature of Jesus as he suffered on the cross. But like many people before me, I had great difficulty trying to achieve this balance. Catholic faith required belief that Jesus' divine intellect and will were always in control. This became a tightrope exercise for me: how could I take seriously that Jesus was really human, which entails limited knowledge, without denying Church doctrine that insists Jesus knew all along that he was God incarnate? Any suggestion that Jesus may have lived with some uncertainty was not acceptable to the guardians of Church doctrine.

I did mentally what I suspect many people have done in dealing with this 'mystery'. I simply acknowledged my belief that Jesus had a divine nature, and at the same time acknowledged that humanly he did not know everything. After all, did not Scripture proclaim that he '*was like us in all things except sin*'?

Juggling the two strands of this 'mystery', the divine nature and the human nature of Jesus, and trying not to lessen belief in one in favor of the other, I found myself contemplating the human reality of Jesus as a man of faith. This was the dawning of an insight that made the deepest impression on me. I started to think: *Jesus really knew what it is like to walk in my shoes.* I had always thought that Jesus with his divine knowledge and divine intellect breezed through life. I had believed that he knew everything and could manage everything according to God's plan. Now I began to think about him as someone who did not know everything and who was more like me, like us, in ways I had never imagined. It took some years for this new thinking to take root in my mind and to become the bedrock of my spiritual life and my relationship with Jesus. In the meantime I kept juggling the theology about Jesus with a divine and a human nature.

Raymond Brown's questions turned upside down my thinking about the resurrection of Jesus. Previously I had believed that Jesus went through his life and endured his suffering on the cross with the certain knowledge that he was God incarnate. Now, pondering Brown's 'What if' questions, I began to imagine Jesus humanly not knowing his divine identity. I began to imagine and think about his death as a supreme and courageous act of faith in the God in whom he trusted. I came to imagine and think that only in death, freed from all human limitation, did Jesus experience the incredible moment of realization: *Wow! This is who I really am! Oh, wow!* And I rejoiced with him.

It was the beginning of my struggle with Church teaching about the two natures of Jesus. However, at the time I thought I had achieved a fine balance. I was not denying the divinity of Jesus as taught by the Church. I was respecting Church teaching that Jesus really was human like us. And I still believed that Jesus' death and resurrection had opened access to God in heaven. I still firmly believed the Church's traditional, mainstream theology of redemption.

After ordination I spent several years teaching in Papua New Guinea. Then in the mid-1970s my congregation invited Armand Nigro SJ to Australia to conduct a twenty-five day renewal program for the Australian MSCs. It was a turn-around experience in my life. For the first time, despite more than fifteen years of religious life behind me, I learned a way of prayer that made sense to me. Nigro taught us how to pray with the Scriptures. Praying with Gospel stories helped me to imagine myself being with Jesus, meeting him, talking with him, interacting with him, listening to him talk to me. Nigro invited us to '*be there, be with, let him* ...' This was a new spiritual experience in which I met Jesus as friend, as companion, as someone with whom I could share my own lived experience. I came to know a Jesus who knew what it was like to experience the ups and downs of human existence.

Most of us who did that renewal program came away from it knowing we had not only met Jesus in a new way, but we had also met ourselves in a new way. We came in touch with our own humanness, much of which had been squeezed out or ossified during our novitiate training. Our priestly formation had produced many self-reliant men out of touch with their own emotions.

About this time, Jim Cuskelly MSC and other MSCs articulated and promoted four movements of what came to be known as a 'Spirituality of the Heart'. I was fortunate to begin working in retreat ministry soon afterwards, and the retreat team further expanded and promoted this spirituality. My new ministry grounded me in a heart spirituality and in convictions that have profoundly influenced my life and everything I have written.

While the movements are generally numbered one to four and may be sequential for people being introduced to them, any one of them might be focused on at any time.

Know yourself, the first movement, is basic to any genuine spirituality. At the retreat center we often quoted the words of Jean Laplace: '*The reason most Christians do not pray properly is that they rarely descend to the bottom of their hearts and remain there*'.

Knowing ourselves operates at many different levels. At one level we might become aware that life is pushing us into a corner or is demanding that we accept the reality of who we are. We need to engage that awareness rather than bury it with noise, busy-ness, distractions, and activity about many other things. No matter how eloquent and theologically correct our prayers may be, they can never be genuine if we are pouring out words while running away from the realities of life and our own personal difficulties. Authentic prayer is impossible if we are not in touch with ourselves, our motivations, our longings, our desires, our fears, our hurts and pains, and anything within and around us to which we are not reconciled or which we resolutely refuse to face. Many people had never been helped to 'descend to the bottom of their hearts and remain there'. I was one of them.

Knowing oneself is not always concerned with the big issues in life, however. At another level, it embraces our everyday experiences, our awareness of moods and attitudes, and our ability to name 'What's going on in me?' when we feel out of sorts, irritable, critical, or weary. When we become aware of 'what's going on in me' and can name it and ponder its causes, we free ourselves from being driven by our feelings or by unconscious attitudes.

The second movement invites us to use whatever we find in the encounters with our own lived experience as stepping stones to the heart of Jesus. We take the reality of our own lives and share it with Jesus as friend and companion. For example, we might imagine asking Jesus, 'Jesus, did you ever feel the way I feel?' 'Did you ever feel misunderstood?' 'Did you ever feel so let-down that you were tempted to give up?' We talk to Jesus about what is going on within and around us. We let him talk to us.

That is what friends do. We try to walk in each other's shoes. We call it empathy. But it can only happen when people truly and trustingly share with one another the secrets, the depths, the realities stirring in their own hearts.

In trusted relationships friends are able to draw us deeper into ourselves, into more honesty about ourselves.

If we want an authentic relationship with Jesus, if we want him to be friend and companion throughout life, we need to know him as someone who understands the human condition. We need to feel we can turn to him in times of both joys and sorrows. We do Jesus a grave disservice if we think, 'Oh, he would never understand what's in my heart. He would never understand my pain, my struggles, my doubts, my darkness. He was God.' Yet that thinking and attitude is commonplace among Christians thanks to centuries of the Church emphasizing the divinity of Jesus.

Armand Nigro's approach to praying the Gospels ideally complemented this second movement. Whereas the Gospel stories had been typically used to prove that Jesus was God incarnate, the invitation now was to use Gospel stories to know Jesus personally on the human level. Whatever the situation, *be there* and be in touch with his feelings, thoughts and emotions. Let him be really human. Respond to his invitation, *'Come and learn of my heart.'*

The third movement flows from the first two movements. In a mutually loving relationship there is the double-sided experience of: *I love and accept you as you are*; and *I am loved and accepted by you as I am*. In our relationship with Jesus this joyful awareness flows from the encounter with the human Jesus as we contemplate gospel stories imaginatively and prayerfully. Coming to a personal conviction that we are loved and accepted for who we are by Jesus is a deeply liberating experience.

A loving relationship, however, also invites or challenges us to be better than we have been, to get our act together, to work on that part of ourselves that we know needs more attention and effort. Genuine friendship invites such growth and expansiveness. So in the development of a deep personal relationship with Jesus, the third movement hopefully leads, as the benefit of genuine friendship can, to resolution of personal issues that need to be addressed and resolved. It can lead to greater self-awareness, better self-understanding, more self-acceptance, and the acceptance of reality.

This movement leads to the awareness that Jesus would offer to everyone the same compassionate friendship we now share with him. We then realize that we should be as compassionately present to others as we have experienced Jesus' compassionate presence with and attitude toward us. Our deepening relationship with Jesus is not to become a cozy and comfortable personal experience. It is not to stop there.

This understanding leads to the fourth movement: deepening the quality of our interactions with others.

More than one hundred and fifty years ago John Henry Newman preached these words in his sermon on Christian Sympathy:

> *I consider that Christians, certainly those who are in the same outward circumstances, are very much more like each other in their temptations, inward diseases, and methods of cure, than they at all imagine. Persons think themselves isolated in the world; they think no one ever felt as they feel. They do not dare to expose their feelings, lest they should find that no one understands them. And thus they suffer to wither and decay what was destined in God's purpose to adorn the Church's paradise with beauty and sweetness. Their "mouth is not opened," as the Apostle speaks, nor their "heart enlarged"; they are "straitened" in themselves, and deny themselves the means they possess of at once imparting instruction and gaining comfort.[1]*

---

[1] Sermon 9. Christian Sympathy. Newman Reader — Works of John Henry Newman. Copyright © 2007 by The National Institute for Newman Studies.

The fourth movement invites us into this awareness of how alike we all are, and to allow this awareness to inspire a compassionate stance towards life and towards other people. This stance must embrace our everyday relationships, any ministry, any arena of social action and any other area of concern for others. We strive to bring the same quality of our relationship with Jesus to all our relationships. We bring our own and his tolerance, understanding, and encouragement to a world, and to a Church, where judgment, prejudice and condemnation are all too prevalent. We commit ourselves to model what Jesus called 'the reign of God' in the world around us. We do this primarily in the way we are present to others. We choose to be present as Jesus would be present. We seek to bring God's unconditional love to others. We choose, as the MSCs express it, '*To be on earth the heart of God*'.

Many people resonate readily with this spirituality of the heart and find the four movements enlightening and fruitful. Some people are less at ease with the spirituality because their spiritual path is more at home with orthodox thinking and reflection on doctrinal truths than with matters of the heart. However, since Jesus is the foundation stone of our Christian faith, and since spiritual wisdom has always proclaimed the need to 'know thyself', it could be reasonably expected that heart spirituality would be appreciated even by Catholics more comfortable with other spiritual paths. I was surprised to discover that this was not so. Again and again, I heard and read comments protesting: *You are denying the divinity of Jesus. You are saying he is only human.* For many Catholics the idea that Jesus might really have been just as human as they are was unwelcome and unthinkable because it could lead people to doubt his divinity.

As those of us in the retreat ministry embraced and implemented this heart spirituality in our own lives while preaching it to others, something became evident to us. We realized that for all of our lives we and others had been steeped in a spirituality that focused on life being a journey *to* a distant God. God was generally considered to be in heaven while we labored in exile here on earth. Aspects of this thinking became clearer as we explored it further. For example, we noticed the way our formal prayers were addressed to God as if God were elsewhere listening in; we carried the belief that we must get our act together and improve ourselves in order to win God's approval and love; we had acquired the belief that the more good we did the more God would love and reward us; we were taught that the spiritual life was a struggle to overcome ourselves because 'our natural tendencies' were a barrier to spiritual growth; life on earth was merely a preparation for the next life with God; none of us could presume we were close to God.

Now, as we steeped ourselves in heart spirituality we came to experience and appreciate that life is a journey *with* God, not a journey *to* God. Deepening our relationship with Jesus led us to experience a profound sense of God's presence with us and God's love for us. God was not distant from us; we were not in exile from God. Heart spirituality had not only deepened our awareness of ourselves, our friendship with Jesus, and our desire to be more compassionate. It also helped us to see the truth of what we had heard from Scripture all our lives, that living in love is really about living *in* God. There was nothing new in that statement, but now we began to take it seriously. In doing so, we found it helpful to emphasize the statement by italicizing the word 'in'. Thus, 'When we live in love, we live *in* God, and God lives *in* us.' For many people that simple emphasis raised their awareness of God's constant presence in their lives in new and profound ways.

We found ourselves asking some pertinent questions. Why do most Christians think they are not close to God? What is the primary task of personal prayer? Is it to talk to an elsewhere God, or is it to deepen personal awareness of and belief in God's presence with us? How should awareness of God's presence with us impact on what we do liturgically? Exploring such questions shaped both my personal spirituality and my ministry in adult faith education in the years ahead.

When I later moved to parish ministry I found parishioners appreciated my efforts to link their own lived experience with Jesus' experience. They welcomed the invitation to enter into the Gospel stories and discover the Jesus with a human heart, and to hear Sunday after Sunday that their lives were a journey *in* and *with* God.

Parishioners encouraged me to write about what they were hearing in my preaching and in adult faith education sessions. Consequently, when I moved to Melbourne in 1992 to begin a ministry in adult faith formation, I published my first book, *God Is Near. Understanding a Changing Church*. The book carried an Imprimatur and a Nihil Obstat from the Archdiocese of Melbourne and was launched by the regional bishop.

To my enormous surprise I then discovered a side of the Catholic Church I had never experienced in twenty three years of priestly ministry. The book was severely attacked by ultra-conservative Catholics who clearly had no interest in or appreciation of the book's basic message that life is a journey *with* God. I was accused of being too easy on people, of not being tough enough on the reality of mortal sin, and of undermining Jesus' full knowledge that he was the Son of God who knew fully the Father's plans for the salvation of the world. The critics found an ally in another regional bishop who later became the archbishop of Melbourne. Unknown to me, the book was sent to Rome for examination by the Congregation for the Doctrine of the Faith. In 1996 the CDF notified the Superior General of the Missionaries of the Sacred Heart in Rome that the book transgressed Church doctrine and was an attack on the Church. The anonymous CDF writer condemned the book's proposition that Jesus lived by faith on the grounds that the divine will was always in control of his humanity.

Shortly before I wrote *God Is Near*, a friend urged me to explore 'the new universe story' as articulated by authors such as Thomas Berry and Brian Swimme. Initially I resisted the advice, saying I was quite content preaching Jesus and spreading the spirituality of the heart in my adult faith formation ministry. My friend persisted and eventually I started to read the literature. Once again I found my religious worldview turned upside down.

From my seminary training I knew that Catholic scripture scholarship did not support a literal reading of the creation stories in the Book of Genesis. However, I had never stopped to consider the theological implications of not taking the accounts literally. Instead, like most Christians, I unreflectively accepted the theological story of a God who locked people out of heaven because of a sin committed by the first humans. Even while my ministry focused on the human Jesus, I continued to believe that he was the incarnation of a God in heaven who had closed access to Himself. I never questioned the lock-out God idea on which salvation was based. I never questioned the notion of a God in heaven who devised a plan to set things right after the sin of the first humans had offended Him so grievously.

As I read the scientific story of the universe and how life unfolded on earth, it was indisputable that the human species did not emerge into a state of paradise, but into a rugged, even hostile, environment. It was also clear that our earliest human ancestors were not capable of making a moral decision that would have caused God to sever contact with humanity.

Major theological questions began to emerge for me. If there was no primeval lock-out, what then of all the theology dependent on taking the lock-out literally? If God had not closed 'the gates of heaven', what happens to all the theology which proclaims that Jesus had to die on a cross for the 'gates' to be opened for us? Is the story of 'the fall' the only story in which we can and must understand the life and teaching of Jesus?

I soon discovered that publicly raising these important and valid questions would find me officially ostracized from the institutional Roman Catholic Church.

1993 - 2000

Throughout the 1990s I conducted many parish-based workshops and seminars on adult faith development along with staff development days for religious education teachers in Catholic elementary and high schools. It became apparent to me that many adults felt uncomfortable with some of the key doctrines of Catholic faith. Teachers especially were ill at ease with major components of the religious education syllabus they were required to teach. Many expressed the ambiguity they often experienced. They felt they were being intellectually dishonest when they were obliged to teach content that conflicted with scientific evidence and with their knowledge about the universe and how life developed on earth.

A typical syllabus contained statements such as, '*Sin and death came into the world when the first man and woman chose to disobey God*'. Teachers rejected on scientific grounds any assertion that the human species had emerged into a state of paradise. They also knew that most of their students shared their thinking on this basic issue. Yet, the *Catechism of the Catholic Church,* published in 1994 contained the definitive statement that, '*The account of the fall in Genesis 3 uses figurative language, but affirms a primeval event, a deed that took place at the beginning of the history of man.*' (# 390)

Elementary school teachers asked how they could be intellectually faithful to what the Catechism and the religious education syllabus required them to teach when even six-year-old children knew that dinosaurs became extinct more than sixty million years before the human species emerged. High school teachers asked how they could respect the Catechism's teaching that a 'fall' at the beginning of human history made 'creation subject to its bondage of decay' when their students could point out that 99.9% of every living species that ever lived on this planet had been annihilated before the human species appeared.

At the dawn of a new millennium the Hubble telescope presented to the world an unprecedented explosion of scientific data about our universe and planet earth's place in it. This provided an understanding of the origin and size of the universe and the origins of earth and the beginning of humanity never known before. Religious education could not ignore this new data if faith was to be grounded solidly in reality. In this new context, educators were looking for intellectual leadership in the difficult task of handing on Catholic and Christian faith.

Traditional Christian teaching about salvation is based on belief in the 'fall' and on belief that access to heaven was denied as a result of the sin of the 'first parents'. To question these foundational beliefs, as I discovered many adults were doing, inevitably led them to question their understanding of the role of Jesus as 'savior'. This was theologically problematic ground for them. They had never been prepared for the dilemma they now faced, and official Church help was not forthcoming. The *Catechism of the Catholic Church* clearly states, '*We cannot tamper with the revelation of original sin without undermining the mystery of Christ.*' (#389). According to Catholic teaching the story of the fall is the only acceptable way to understand salvation and the role of Jesus. The guardians of Catholic belief knew no other way to present Jesus to the world except as the savior who freed humanity from the bondage of original sin.

It was the dilemma facing Catholic parents and educators that led me to publish *Tomorrow's Catholic. Understanding God and Jesus in a New Millennium*, (1997). I wrote the book as a Catholic priest, grounded in a heart spirituality, who wanted to bring the message of Jesus to the modern world. I wrote it as an adult faith educator keen to present important theological ideas in non-academic language. My intent was to show that there is another story in our scriptures and in our Christian tradition about God. It is not the story of God disconnected from creation and from humanity. Rather, it is a story about God as a universal presence, 'charging' all that exists. And there is another story about Jesus as savior. It is not a story about Jesus bridging a supposed disconnection between God and humanity. It is the story of Jesus who wanted to open people's minds to God's presence with them in their everyday lives. It is the story of Jesus who wanted people to draw upon God's abiding presence and create the 'kingdom of God' here on earth. I wanted people to understand that the very same Spirit of God that moved in and sustained Jesus is present in every human person whether they are aware of it or not.

Six months after the book was published I was summoned to the office of the newly appointed, ultra-conservative archbishop of Melbourne.

At the meeting, the archbishop handed me a ten page document he had written. It consisted primarily of quotes from the *Catechism of the Catholic Church*. In the document I was accused of denying Church doctrine, specifically the divinity of Jesus and the reality of God as a trinity of persons. Another concern was that I had called into question Catholic teaching that good people only enter heaven because 'Christ died for our sins'. The archbishop was also concerned that I had quoted some non-Catholic authors in the book. He informed me that, henceforth, I was not to preach publicly on the topics of Incarnation, Redemption and the Trinity. I was informed that the Catholics of Melbourne would be notified the following week that my book was in error and was not to be sold in Catholic bookshops. He provided me with a draft copy of the notification to Catholics in the archdiocese. The archbishop insisted that

I must answer to him personally and that I should respond to his concerns within seven days if I wanted to avoid this public announcement.

My religious superiors objected strongly to the archbishop's public condemnation a week later of my theology and the public banning of the book when the Church's own recently published due processes of theological investigation were ignored by the archbishop. My Provincial sought a meeting with the Archbishop to discuss a belated, but proper, objective investigation of the book. The three MSCs present at the meeting, myself included, agreed that I would submit the book to a panel of theologians and that I would incorporate their suggestions into a new edition of the book. However, when my provincial asked the archbishop what would happen if the panel of theologians should differ from the archbishop's opinion on a particular issue, we were told to clearly understand that he had the final say: the book had to be re-written according to what he judged to be correct theology. Knowing that the archbishop had effectively made up his mind on the matter and had publicly made known his views, we saw no point in pursuing this course. The MSC provincial council consequently withdrew me from ministry in the Melbourne archdiocese.

I then became known as a priest 'banned by his archbishop'. Predictably, bishops in other Australian dioceses cancelled work I had been engaged to conduct in their dioceses.

My MSC superiors advised me to consult with a number of academic theologians in various states of Australia about the book and how I might have avoided the trouble it caused. I did so willingly, but could not have predicted how the advice I received from each of three eminent theologians would determine the path I would follow in the next phase of my ministry as an adult faith educator.

One theologian advised me, "Do what the archbishop is asking. Sign on the dotted line to what he wants you to say so that you can stay in ministry and continue teaching."

Another stated, "The task of a Catholic theologian is not to change the Creed but to bring our contemporary knowledge of the universe into harmony with the Creed."

The third said, "Doctrine cannot change. You cannot call yourself a Catholic and call doctrine into question. Doctrine shapes the identity and self-understanding of the Church."

I found, and still find it regrettable, that academic theologians in the Catholic Church will not or cannot publicly engage the central issues raised in *Tomorrow's Catholic*.

As an adult faith educator I had witnessed the urgent need to bring adult understanding of God and Jesus into harmony with contemporary knowledge about the age and size of the universe and how life developed on earth. Faith must be built on reality. I lamented the widespread experience of so many adults who felt they could not relate with Jesus and who could no longer believe the concept of a God who locked people out of heaven. What I lamented even more was that Catholic Church leadership strenuously resisted any alternate 'story' or context in which to articulate religious faith. It preferred to ignore what was becoming a matter of urgency for faith formation in the twenty-first century - that there must be ways to present God and Jesus to the world today that do not require people to ignore reality and to suspend reason.

After reflection on the collective opinion of the theologians I had met and on the fact that I had been banned from teaching on Catholic property, I had no wish to continue ministry within the narrow parameters that had been set. The final straw for me came when an archbishop cancelled work for which I had been engaged, telling the organizer of the proposed event, "I do not know Michael personally; I have not read his book; I have nothing against him, but I cannot afford to have him speak in my archdiocese when he has been banned in Melbourne."

I resigned from priestly ministry and religious life at the end of 1998, grateful to the Missionaries of the Sacred Heart for their ongoing support and encouragement, and with what will be a life-long gratitude for their spirituality of the heart.

2000 - 2014

An unexpected door opened in 1999 when, through an extraordinary act of generosity, I was able to make contact with like-minded Catholics and other Christians in the United States. The American experience further convinced me of the need to present Jesus and his message in a way that does not rely on the traditional story of a fall and a lock-out God.

Subsequently, I wrote a book with the intentionally provocative title, *Is Jesus God? Finding Our Faith* (2001). The book was intended as an exercise in adult faith formation and development. It was based on the premise that faith should be reasonable, not merely dogmatic. Any adult Christian should be able to give a reasoned explanation why the Christian religion insists that Jesus must have a divine nature that makes him essentially different from any other human person.

The reality, however, is that most Christians are not able to give a reasoned explanation. They simply accept the doctrine of the Church as absolute truth and do not question it. They have no knowledge of the historical events, the worldview, or the religious questions of the first four centuries that led the Christian Church to decide that Jesus had to be identified with God in a way the rest of humanity is not. The story they know well is that God so loved the world that He sent his Son to die for our sins, and surely you are not going to deny that! Several personal factors had also motivated me to write *Is Jesus God?*

One factor was my conviction that the issues I raised in *Tomorrow's Catholic* were not going away. Silencing me with quotes from the Catechism merely avoided pertinent issues that challenged the assumptions and worldview which ground traditional redemption theology. I knew from discussions with teachers and other adults that they were looking for an articulation of faith that did not rely on assumptions

and assertions that flatly contradicted scientific knowledge
and common sense.

A second personal factor was my reflection on the
mystery of God as I absorbed the scientific data about our
universe and how life developed on earth. Images from the
Hubble telescope did more to expand my notion of God
than any theology I had ever read. I wondered why, at the
beginning of the twenty-first century, anyone exposed to all
the data available about the expansiveness of our universe
and earth's place in it would not be open to expanding their
notion of God beyond what they acquired from Scripture
written in pre-scientific times. Was it not time for our faith
to move beyond the understanding of a heavenly God overseeing earth as the center-piece of His creation?

I looked for another understanding of God that was
faithful to Christian tradition and which reflected our contemporary knowledge of the universe and our place in it. It
was not difficult to find. It is an understanding Christianity
has always had. God is everywhere. God is the sustainer of
all that exists. Nothing can exist outside of God. God is
the Ground of All Being. Gregory of Nyssa in the 4th century expressed this traditional thinking well when he asked,
"Who could be so simple minded as not to believe that the
Divine is present in everything, pervading, embracing and
penetrating it?"

While this understanding of God, the Divine Presence,
has always been an essential part of our Christian tradition, it has been given little more than lip-service by the
institution which has favored the notion of God found
in Scripture. There is much to be gained institutionally by
claiming to have unique insight into the thoughts and opinions of this God. The Church taught for many centuries,
that only Christians could gain access to this God through

faith in Jesus and entrance into the Church. There is much to be gained institutionally by the claim that adherence to this institution is essential for salvation. On the other hand, there is much to lose institutionally if people follow the preaching of Jesus and realize that the Divine Presence is always within them, is given daily expression in their lives, and should be listened to.

In the book I sought to challenge adult Christians who want to proclaim in the twenty-first century that Jesus must have a divine nature that we do not possess. The challenge is to articulate the reasoning process that leads them to this conclusion. However, they must do so as people informed by a contemporary understanding of the universe. They may not claim that the human species emerged into a state of paradise. They may not literalize the story of 'original sin' at humanity's beginning. They may not rely on a notion of God who withheld friendship and forgiveness, a notion of God that would be unacceptable to Jesus. They may not disregard Jesus' conviction and teaching that God's presence was with people before and during his lifetime. They may not deny Christianity's claim that whoever lives in love lives *in* God and God lives *in* them. They are to avoid those mistakes because they are miss-takes on reality. Now articulate the reasonable grounds on which their faith conclusions about Jesus are based.

I know of no Roman Catholic theologian who holds an official teaching position in the Catholic Church nor any member of the institutional hierarchy who has attempted this task publicly. It is clear that any academic or ecclesial leader who made the attempt without resorting to a pre-scientific worldview would inevitably cast doubt on foundational Christian theological premises. Since no one wants to do this publicly, the doctrine that focuses on the Christ who died for our sins and opened the gates of heaven remains publicly unquestioned for fear of condemnation and reprisal.

In June 2000, the Congregation for the Doctrine of the Faith issued the Declaration, *Dominus Iesus,* which asserted that *'Above all else, it must be firmly believed that the Church, a pilgrim now on earth, is necessary for salvation.'* (#20)

The Declaration confirmed the reactionary theological trend in the Catholic Church for the previous twenty years. It exemplified the Vatican's retreat from engagement with the modern world into the security of dogmatism.

The institutional Church, having professed its readiness in the 1960s to engage the modern world, now under the control of Pope John Paul II and Cardinal Ratzinger had adopted a siege mentality. *Dominus Iesus* was written for bishops, many of them appointed by John Paul II. It sought to prevent any scrutiny of the theology that allowed the institutional Church to see itself as *'necessary for salvation'.* It also presented the strategy for protecting the institutional Church from voices that had become louder since Vatican II, voices asserting that the institutional Church in its identity, governance, teaching and practice was a long way removed from Jesus' preaching about the 'kingdom of God'. The tactic was simple: authoritatively quote Scripture and strenuously re-state Church dogma; insist that Scripture and dogma are beyond questioning; stress what must be *'firmly believed and taught'.* This tactic, which is still in place, allows bishops to silence anyone who dares to question official Church teaching. It effectively shields bishops from any need to engage the faith questions of adult Catholics who are looking to leadership to help them build their faith on reality.

In many aspects there was nothing new in *Dominus Iesus.* The document revealed the theological mindset that has governed the Catholic Church for centuries: God had a plan for salvation; Jesus died for our sins; Jesus founded the Church; Jesus '*alone bestows divine life to all humanity and to every person*'; no one can be in communion with God '*except through Christ, by the working of the Holy Spirit.*' This dogmatism allowed the Vatican to demand that '*The Catholic faithful are required to profess that there is an historical continuity - rooted in the apostolic succession - between the Church founded by Christ and the Catholic Church.*'

In the section on 'the relationship between the kingdom of God, the kingdom of Christ, and the Church', bishops are warned about 'one-sided accentuations' which emphasize 'bearing witness to and serving the kingdom'. In other words, they are to be wary of suggestions that the Church as institution is answerable to Jesus' preaching about the kingdom of God. They are to be on guard against suggestions that the 'kingdom' of which Jesus speaks is more universally inclusive and more important than the '*kingdom of the Church*'. The dangers of such suggestions are:

> *First, they are silent about Christ: the kingdom of which they speak is 'theocentrically' based, since, according to them, Christ cannot be understood by those who lack Christian faith, whereas different peoples, cultures, and religions are capable of finding common ground in the one divine reality, by whatever name it is called. For the same reason, they put great stress on the mystery of creation, which is reflected in the diversity of cultures and beliefs, but they keep silent about the mystery of redemption. Furthermore, the kingdom, as they understand it, ends up either leaving very little room for the Church or undervaluing the Church in reaction to a presumed 'ecclesiocentrism' of the past and because they consider the Church herself only a sign, for that matter a sign not without ambiguity.*

This section highlights the recurring fear in the Declaration that if people take seriously God's presence as a universal reality, accessible to everyone, then the Church's claim to have unique access to revelation and the unique granting of divine life to people will be undermined.

The statement about those who 'put great stress on the mystery of creation' pinpoints one of the clearest challenges to Church teaching in modern times. Scholarship dealing with 'the mystery of creation' relies on and accepts scientific data about the origins of the universe, of earth, and of life on earth. This scholarship inevitably raises questions about the worldview in which the Church's redemption theology and its teaching about Christ who reconnected humanity with an elsewhere God are grounded. Bishops have no way of addressing these questions. Their only recourse is to rely on authoritative statements such as that which follows the paragraph quoted above from *Dominus Iesus*: '*These theses are contrary to Catholic faith because they deny the unicity of the relationship which Christ and the Church have with the kingdom of God.*' End of story; no discussion. Bishops have the authority to silence anyone who attempts to raise questions, ideas and even factual evidence in support of an alternate way to understand Jesus and his importance for humanity.

In the Introduction to *Is Jesus God?* I wrote:

> *I predict that in this new century many committed Christians will wonder how Christianity could have stayed embedded so long in the idea that Jesus had to be interpreted as a god-figure who came down to earth to redress a terrible mistake made by the first human beings. Increasing disenchantment with institutional church structures and liturgy reliant on an outdated theological framework is inevitable.*

Fourteen years later I am not surprised by the increasing disenchantment among Christians of many denominations who have rejected the outdated, traditional, Christian theological framework. Adults expect and want their Church leaders to articulate faith that can withstand rigorous examination. When such an articulation is not forthcoming, many people abandon formal religion and seek other ways to live their faith. They choose to explore and embrace an understanding of God that is well beyond the limited notions of God found in Scripture and in Church doctrine. They continue to express their allegiance to Jesus and his message while carrying disappointment that Church leadership is failing to bring the person and teaching of Jesus into engagement with the modern world.

What many adult Christians are experiencing in their own personal reflections, in their homes, in their adult faith-sharing groups, and in their Church communities is not a movement to undermine faith. It is not anti-Christian. It is not anti-Church. It is most definitely not anti-Jesus. The sincere questioning that many adults experience arises from the conviction that the primary task of their church is to be a light to the world by preaching Jesus' message without compromise.

My personal experience of questioning important aspects of my Catholic faith did not start with and was not motivated by a desire to be a liberal, theological non-conformist. Rather, my questioning was prompted by a spirituality in which I met Jesus as friend and companion. The questioning increased with my growing appreciation that Jesus has a message that the world urgently needs to hear. My conviction deepened that the Church must do what Jesus did. The Church must affirm the Divine in all people, respect the Divine in all people, listen to the Divine in all people, and challenge everyone to create a better world in which the Divine would be clearly manifest in our religious, social, political, economic and environmental systems.

I found myself asking three important questions. Why has Christianity never done this in its 2000 year history? For what did Jesus really want to be remembered? How can Christianity best bring Jesus and his message to the modern world?

My ongoing ministry as an adult faith educator has focused on those questions. I came to appreciate how fearful many Christians, including, I suspect, many bishops in the Catholic Church, are of questioning traditional theology about Jesus as Redeemer of the world. They cannot entertain the thought that doctrine can be questioned. They fear their faith will collapse, that the Church will lose its identity, and that any questioning of Scripture will undermine its role in determining belief. They do not have a story or perspective in which to rebuild and articulate their faith.

I have come to realize that a new articulation of Christian faith does exist. It starts with the recognition that God is Inexpressible Mystery beyond all Scriptural and doctrinal descriptions. It develops the understanding that this Mystery is at work in all places and at all times in the development and the on-going evolution of the human species. It tells a story of God-always-with-us and always given voice within the human community. It helps people to discern how that presence and that voice are given proper human expression, and how they are ignored to our detriment. It respects the human wisdom arising from that presence and that voice in all places and in all cultures. It acknowledges that men and women everywhere are children of God when they are merciful, when they work for justice and peace, when they treat others with dignity and respect. It tells a story about the dignity of a life species able to acknowledge that it gives expression to God at work in the universe.

Central and indispensable to this articulation of Christian faith is the human reality of Jesus. I believe there is no way to construct a credible Christian faith in the twenty-first century if Jesus' humanity continues to be overshadowed and undermined by focusing on the man-god who wins salvation. The humanness of Jesus must be presented as our common human story, the story of the Mystery that is God, coming to expression in human form. Christians must be educated anew to focus on this understanding of Jesus and themselves. This focus will allow all followers of Jesus to hear him say, "See me, a human expression of the Divine Power at work in the universe; this is who and what you are. Believe this good news and make the world a better place." Such a focus could return the Church to its primary task of bringing the inspired teaching of Jesus to center stage and to proclaim to the world: "See, this is how we are to live in relationship with one another. This is the way."

My experience in spirituality and adult faith formation ministry has revealed that the faith of most adult Roman Catholics I have met mirrored my own personal experience up to the time of my ordination. They know the theology about Jesus the Christ, the man-god, but few have a personal relationship with Jesus, heart to heart.

In April 1992, the Australian Catholic Bishops Conference released a document on *The Decade of Evangelisation 1990-2000*. The document contained the following remarkable statement:

> *Perhaps the greatest task may well be that of inspiring our active Catholics to come to know Jesus, to be converted to him, to make him central to their lives, to imitate him and to share their experience of him with others.*

In this statement the bishops implicitly acknowledged that *active Catholics* do *not* know Jesus, do *not* make him central to their lives, and do *not* imitate him. I believe it was also an admission that the Catholic Church's presentation of Jesus to committed Catholics has left them unable to relate with him as someone who has experienced the everyday ups and downs of human experience. Yet when an attempt is made to address this, using gospel stories and imaginative prayer forms, bishops world-wide, supported by the Congregation for the Doctrine of the Faith, denounce this approach with the charge that it undermines Church doctrine about Jesus' divine will and divine knowledge. According to doctrine Jesus is only to be remembered as someone fundamentally unlike the rest of us. That makes it very difficult to *know* him and to *imitate* him.

We should *know* him. We should relate with him as friend.

PART 5

Friends in Conversation

"Hello, Jesus."

"Hello, Michael. How are you today?"

"I'm not really sure. That's why I want to spend time with you. I have many thoughts and feelings I'd like to share with you, but I don't know where to start."

"That's not unusual when you're talking with me, is it? Why not do what you usually do, just jump in somewhere and see where it takes us."

"OK…

"I found myself thinking about you this morning when I reflected on the prayer workshop I conducted last weekend. The workshop went well, and as I've told you before, when things go well, I often think of you having good days and good times when you were able to get through to people. But it doesn't take much for my mind and my emotions to be pushed in another direction when I start to consider the enormous task of trying to change deeply embedded religious beliefs and practices, not in a small group as I had on the weekend, but in the Christian Church in general. I can easily become discouraged and start asking myself, 'Who do you think you are?' So I just need to share that with you, once again, knowing you understand."

"Oh, yes! 'Who do you think you are?!' I heard that time and again! And I had no easy answer. No acceptable qualifications. Just my conviction that God's Spirit moved me."

"But personal conviction can run into a brick wall. I think that's what discourages me. People constantly affirm that I have something worthwhile to say, something that resonates with common-sense and truth and the spiritual stirrings within them. Yet, despite the fact that it gives people hope for meaningful religious belief and practice, there is monumental institutional resistance to it."

"We've been through this before, haven't we? You and I have something in common, Michael. You, too, will die without seeing the widespread changes you'd like to see. And I think the task of achieving them is more difficult in these times than when I was alive on earth. Today there are even more powerful vested interests resistant to the changes the human community needs to undertake if God's influence is to take hold."

"I guess you hoped that your message might have taken a better hold in the human community than what you see two thousand years after your death."

"Yes, I thought that my teaching might inspire a movement that would gradually spread. I didn't expect it to happen quickly, but I did hope that one day people would finally come to see that violence, greed, domination and fear are not the way to demonstrate God's presence and influence in human affairs. Justice, compassion, mercy, acceptance, peace - that's what people long for. And that's the message I wanted the movement to proclaim courageously and faithfully to the world, just as Judaism was called to do."

"It could have, should have come through the Christian religion, but we won't go there again! At least not just now. There are other thoughts arising from the weekend and from other workshops that I'd like to discuss with you.

"Let me start with death. I've been utterly fascinated by group discussions and sharing on this topic recently. I've come to believe that the way we think about death in the twenty-first century could provide a new window to our understanding of God and a new start for theology. I know that would sound strange to most people, but it makes sense of my experience. Growing up Catholic, I imagined death as a journey to the heavens where I would be met by God Himself who would then judge whether or not I was worthy enough to be granted entrance. What I had been taught about God determined how I imagined what would happen when I died. I know this imagination was and still is shared by many Christians.

"But, as happened again last weekend, when I invite people to share their thoughts on what they imagine will happen when they die, almost no one is in that imagination any more. Instead, people talk about transformation into existence beyond three dimensions, about transformation of energy, about transformation into conscious awareness of the oneness of everything. Inevitably, people struggle with words, but there is consensus that death is not the end of us, that our human mode of existence gives way to freedom from limitation and to participation in on-going existence beyond human images and human understanding.

"When I invite sharing on what their thinking implies about meeting God in death, many people say they envisage a transformation into the presence of an Ultimate Reality that permeates everything that exists and holds everything in existence.

"I realize that you can't break through into my limited human understanding and reveal all you now know, but I'd like to explore with you something of your experience of death and whether it resonates with what many people are imagining today.

"So, an easy question. What happened to you when you died?"

"I have no words to describe what happens in death, but what I can say certainly resonates with what you are hearing from people. Death released me from all human and all three-dimensional limitations. The best I can say in human terms is that I entered the most glorious, awesome, fullness of reality. I was transformed into full participation with the

One, with the Indescribable. I knew immediately that I was part of Oneness, one with everyone and everything that has ever and will ever exist. I experienced death as birth into full awareness of the Reality we call God."

"It was not like meeting Someone, God, and being welcomed into heaven?"

"No. Not at all. That was the big surprise for me! It's far more wonderful than that. This is the ultimate experience of God we are talking about. God is Universal Reality, expansive beyond any limits, embracing everything that exists. The human concept of God as a Someone is helpful in the human, three-dimensional world, but beyond that world it is meaningless or at least unhelpful. God is not constrained by the limitations of space and time the way a human 'someone' is.

"It's not surprising that people believe that their limited human notions of God govern reality beyond death. It happened with me. I fully expected a 'father' God to embrace me in death. That's the God I humanly knew. But, as I said, the great surprise was to discover not a father figure, but Infinite Reality into which I was transformed when released from human limitations."

"I understand that what you are describing about death is a universal experience, one for all humans, not an experience unique to you."

"Most definitely. Keep remembering that death is the human experience of encountering the Ultimate Mystery. It is the common human experience, not just my experience."

"In the discussions I mentioned, people seem to have no problem accepting that what they expect to happen to them when they die is no different from what would always happen to people, even those who lived long before you. However, such thinking creates a major problem for

Christian theology which maintains that your resurrection was a unique event in human history, that no man or woman who died before you had access to God."

"There will be a problem as long as Church leaders, theologians and preachers continue to believe that God is a deity who resides in the heavens."

"The discussions about death point to a radically different insight into who or what God is. It seems to me, then, that it would be advisable to start our theological thinking in the twenty-first century with an appreciation of this Infinite Reality rather than with the concept of God we grew up with."

"I think that would be advisable. It would give you an appreciation of the profound mystery that God really is. It would also lead to a far deeper understanding of God's presence in the human community. If people understood God as the Ultimate Reality that permeates all existence, everywhere, they would no longer imagine God being here and not there, in this person and not in that person, in these sacred writings and not in other sacred writings. Hopefully they would discard altogether their narrow, limited human notions of God being absent or being a heavenly overseer or a Someone withholding forgiveness. These are all human notions that have no meaning or relevance in the realm of God beyond human life. Yes, start with the God I experienced in death, the God people in your discussion groups expect to meet in death. You could use that new-found appreciation as a lens or filter through which to view human experience and events."

"Starting with this more expansive, more mysterious notion of God, God present everywhere and in all things, helps me to appreciate that humanity has always given particular, wonderful expression to God. I've come to think that we are God expressed in human form. I like that, but I sense many Christians are afraid to think we have such dignity. They have been taught to believe that you and you alone were God expressed in human form."

"That's such a pity. I never believed or taught that. Every person gives human expression to God, the Ultimate Reality. God's presence and activity came to expression not only in and through me but also in and through every man and woman who recognizes and honors the dignity of humanity. They reveal God's presence in human society. God comes to expression in every person who loves, everyone, without exception."

"I find this understanding wonderfully expansive, encouraging and challenging. Most people, though, still want to hold onto their notion of God as a personal being. For many who engage this new approach it is their biggest struggle. It's as if their heads tell them one thing, but their hearts tell them another and they want to hold onto the notion of God deeply instilled in them through exposure to Scripture, Church teaching, liturgy and prayer practices."

"I don't think it's a case of head against heart. It's always difficult for people to shift from a belief system they have been exposed to all their lives and taught never to question. As I discovered, conversion is very difficult because it turns upside down people's thoughts about God and how they are in relationship with God. This type of change requires a lot of time and patience."

"And, of course, Christians look to you and see that you spoke of God in personal terms. I'm often asked about the 'Our Father' and how that type of prayer fits in this new thinking."

"When I was alive on earth I liked to think of God as a loving parent. I frequently urged my listeners to think of God that way. I would still encourage people to do so, but I would ask them to keep in mind that they are using their limited human experience to point to God, a mysterious Reality. They are not describing God. That cannot be done in human terms. They are simply using language and images and ideas that help them to relate with and trust whatever God is. Any familiar terms that people use such as father or mother, and the personal pronouns that go with those terms are only pointers to the Indescribable.

"Invoking God as father or mother can help to establish a relationship of trust with God and to cast out fear. However, the terms should not be used to suggest that God is a Someone who acts like a loving parent overseeing all of creation. When that notion of God prevails, as happened in my own religion, it produces the concept of a God who has opinions about all sorts of issues, who ponders what to do next, who thinks about whether to forgive or not. I grew up with the idea of God as a heavenly overseer, a God in control of everything that happened. I tried to balance that idea with my personal experience that God was like the Breath of Life, present everywhere. Humanly, like all humans before and after me, I struggled with who or what God really is."

"But you never struggled with the conviction that God is to be trusted."

"No. Never. That particular conviction was deeply embedded in me, even as a Jew struggling with the idea that God could be punishing and was to be feared. I think the same conviction is embedded in every child. The trouble is that as children are exposed to the unquestioned authority of adults, to religion, to culture, to suffering, they come to mistrust the stirrings of God's Presence within them. They are led to conceive of God primarily as a deity who rules the world from heaven. They begin to look over their shoulders, fearful of the heavenly God and the way that God is said to control whatever happens to everyone."

"I taught that concept of God to children in the 1960s. Many of us did so when we taught religion in elementary school classes. We filled small minds with the Catechism and theologically 'correct' answers, but we never nurtured the children's awareness of God's presence in them. We didn't know how to. We only knew how to teach religion.

"Religion distracted all of us from focusing on and trusting our own personal experience of God's presence within us. Religion grounded me in the Scriptural and doctrinal concept of an external God who revealed Himself to some people and who sent you from heaven to restore access to Himself. For most of my life I prayed to that God. Sunday after Sunday I heard prayers addressed to a God who I believed noticed my presence and was pleased by it. I thanked that God for all the good things in my life.

"Now I no longer believe in that God of my religion.

"It's an amazing turn-around in my life and in my faith, I'm grateful for all the influences that have led me to think differently.

"Yet the fact is that many Christians would think I have been misled and that I am undermining the foundations of Christian belief."

"Well, you should not be surprised by that, surely. You *are* undermining the foundations of traditional Christian belief! But the good news is that you know many other people no longer subscribe to traditional religion's notion of God either. You know they are looking for a more believable understanding of God. one that resonates with the contemporary worldview."

"Yes, but the shift in thinking raises a significant concern for many of them. They are uncertain how this new understanding of God impacts on their understanding of and respect for Scripture if they do not believe anymore in a God who speaks from the heavens and gives selected people His definitive word on a wide range of topics."

"There is no need to discard Scripture. Rather, the need is to understand how the 'voice' of God is heard within the human community. Let us be quite clear. God does not speak, period. People need to stop imagining a God who can simultaneously listen to and speak every human language because they think God can do anything. That might have been how people, myself included, thought about God two thousand years ago. But that is not the reality of God, and people should know better in the twenty-first century. Rather than imagine a God who speaks from the heavens, consider that the 'voice' people hear comes from within themselves. It is the voice of goodness and truth, of co-operation, of possibility, of expansiveness, of sharing, of creativity. It is the voice of love and compassion.

"Whenever anyone reads about someone in Scripture claiming to hear God speak, even if it is presented as coming from the clouds, they should understand that it is really what I called 'the Spirit of the Lord' coming from within the person making the claim. Everyone carries this voice deep within them. That was true of the prophets; it was true of me; it is true of everyone. If anyone wants to understand it as the voice of God, they should know that this a voice embedded in every newborn baby. People need to grow in awareness of this voice within them and learn to trust it."

"Yet Scripture presents many different and contradictory voices. Some make God seem vindictive, violent and mean-spirited."

"I was well aware of those different voices when I was growing up in Nazareth. I found it puzzling that some synagogue leaders gave equal weight to all the voices. Fortunately there were wiser people in the community who recognized that God's voice came to expression in individuals within their own particular personalities, cultures, interests, learning and worldview. My father was a wise influence on me. He taught me not to take everything in our Scriptures at face value. He was fond of saying that God works in and through what God has to work with. I learned from him and others that discernment is needed when people engage ideas, opinions, cultural laws and religious decrees in Scripture. They are all of human origin. I learned to discern what gives true expression to the Spirit of the Lord at work in the human community."

"You're reminding me of how often I hear people recall significant people in their lives, such as their mothers or a grandparent telling them not to believe everything the Church teaches. There is a depth of spiritual wisdom that surfaces sometimes in the most unlikely people."

"Yes. That's what I experienced with my father.

"I would have expected that two thousand years later, humanity would have benefited more from this wisdom in people and the insights it brings to light."

"No. Unfortunately, religion still locks people into the idea of the external God who chose certain men to consign to writing exactly what God wanted written. Religion still promotes the idea of a God in control of everything. It encourages blind faith in what Scripture and the Church says and distrusts personal and communal wisdom."

"Yes, but the insightful voices of mothers and fathers and grandparents and many others are breaking through more and more, aren't they? Many people no longer give credence to the traffic controller notion of God. They have abandoned belief in a God who allows this or that to happen or who asks someone to carry a burden. Isn't that so?"

"That is so, but the trouble is that most people I meet still want to believe that God is caring and is interested in their well-being. Dare we say that God doesn't care about us and has no interest in what happens here on earth? Does God care about horrifying events like the Holocaust or the widespread suffering and poverty in this world?"

"Questions like that stem from the human need to be known and loved. Religious people look to their human, personal notion of God to fulfill that need. They use their humanly limited notion of God to explain significant events. They talk about God as Love, as Person, as a Compassionate Being, and this leads them to think of God as a *person* who, therefore, must be interested in and cares about human well-being. They need to accept the reality that God is beyond all human concepts and human modes of behavior. It's time to stop boxing God into human, three-dimensional notions of a personal being located somewhere in the heavens who thinks and feels the way a human person might.

"People want God to care about the brutality and violence in the world? They want God to care about suffering? They want God to love them and tell them they are precious and deeply loved? Well, the reality is that they need to do it themselves! Why don't people understand that? *They* are to care; *they* are to stop the suffering that arises from human deceit and misuse of power. Whatever God is - always beyond human knowing - humans give expression to this Ultimate Mystery in their loving, their care, their interest, their desire to make the earth a better place for all. That's the whole point of being human. People need to stop badgering an imaginary listening God and start to work on themselves. They are human, personal expressions of God. If they are not committed to living that reality then God's presence and effectiveness in the world are nullified."

"There's a widespread sense today that the business-as-usual way of doing things is failing us. It is not working in our social, political, economic and religious systems, and it is certainly not working in our care for the environment. I guess you would identify that new consciousness with God's presence among us, urging us to wake up and find better ways to manifest God's presence in the world. But as you mentioned earlier, there are powerful vested interests that resist any alternative approaches or solutions to the many problems we face as a human community. It's what you experienced all over again. I find myself wondering whether you would be any more effective today with your message than you were two thousand years ago."

"I think I would be. As a balance to those powerful vested interests, you have information and technologies for engaging peoples' minds and imagination that did not exist when I was alive. You have instant communication across the planet. Your sciences give you a wonderfully expansive window to the Divine. There is an emerging sense of responsibility and concern for the earth. My message about God's presence in all things would be enhanced by what you have at your disposal. I think God's voice among you today has the possibility of being heard in a way that was not possible when I was alive.

"Two thousand years ago we had such limited knowledge of the cosmos and our place in it. You are now exploring the universe and have a wealth of knowledge about how it unfolded and how it operates. Accordingly, your understanding of God ought to be more expansive than that of people of my lifetime. I would expect that many people in the twenty-first century would be attuned to a more expansive notion of God's presence throughout the universe.

"I also think that the history of human failure over the past two thousand years to achieve anything bearing resemblance to the kingdom of God on earth may well be the wake-up call for human society to do better in the future. People might be more sensitive now to the poor state of human affairs and be more receptive to hear what I really preached about two thousand years ago.

"Would anything in your preaching be different today?"

"In some ways it would, especially in terms of understanding the mystery of God. In keeping with what we discussed a moment ago, I would suggest that people try to conceive of God in terms of the Oneness of everything. I would urge them to think big, to be expansive and to be thoroughly inclusive of everything that exists when they wonder where God is.

"I would also seek to engage other religions. I would try to work with the religions of the world and urge them to operate beyond any institutional claims of exclusive access to the mysterious reality they call 'God' and any claims to speak authoritatively on behalf of God. I would emphasize that people and governments throughout the world must work together to establish a new order of relationships based on mutual care, justice, and respect."

"I cannot imagine that you would change your basic teaching at all."

"Definitely not. It will stand the test of time if it correctly gives expression to the Spirit of God at work in creation. The message God conveyed through me expressed what I believe to be the best way for men and women to live in justice and peace. It is how God can be given proper human expression. It is the way for the kingdom of God to be established on earth. There is nothing more important for humans to understand than my message because without its implementation there will be no lasting peace on earth. Non-Christians and non-religious people may reject some aspects of my message, but

I believe they would agree that a new order of relationships is essential if humanity is to thrive, not just barely survive, into the future."

"I can imagine you saying repeatedly, as you once did, 'Seek the kingdom of God; go sell whatever you have; seek the only treasure that lasts'."

"Oh, there's a lot more you would hear me saying again! It's there in your Gospels: be merciful, be peacemakers, mourn with those who are suffering, do not be proud-hearted, set your hearts and minds on justice and fairness, share, be neighbor, know God is always with you and is not to be feared, act towards others as you would want others to act towards you."

"There are many Christians who focus on you and your message, but the institutional Church seems far more concerned with seeing you as the Christ figure in the context of a very restrictive notion of God. It makes those Christians wonder whether the Church as an institution has a future."

"Oh, it has a future, as all religions have. But it should stop emphasizing that life beyond death is the fundamentally important issue. Religions have no control over what happens to people when they die. Life beyond death takes care of itself, believe me. Religions should not make it the focus of human existence or what religion is primarily about. Religion should be concerned with what Judaism recognized: the need to create human communities and to promote human interactions that reflect the presence of the Spirit of God within and among all humanity.

"When religious people grasp that fundamental truth about religion, they will begin to focus on the quality of life for every person and every living thing here on earth. They will find a way to work together on the monumental agenda of helping the human community to work together so that humanity can free itself from its own self-destructive forces, attitudes and actions. And when they begin to do that, they will discover a new experience of God-with-them. They will discover that there is no need to lock their understanding of God into narrow intellectual boxes. They will abandon their need for theological certainty, and learn to *live* the mystery and the wonder of what it really means to be human."

"One of the theological certainties for Christians, of course, concerns you. Most Christians would protest vehemently at the suggestion that you are not the unique human incarnation of God in heaven. They would believe that such a suggestion demeans you and strips away your importance and your relevance. If you are not the unique 'Son of God' who 'saved the world' from eternal disconnection from God, why should anyone take notice of you?"

"Let them go back to my teaching and look at what I so clearly tried to do. I tried to affirm people in their intimate connection with the Mystery they call God in their ordinary, everyday living. Everyone is a bearer of this Mystery! I wanted people to know and own this wonderful truth about themselves, and then to use it for the good of humanity. There is no need for a Son of God or a divine savior figure to free humanity from disconnection from God or to appease a God withholding forgiveness. Disconnection from God is impossible.

"Turning me into a savior figure doubtless served someone's interests, but it was not part of my message or anything I believed about myself. Was I not clear enough? Did I not sufficiently spell out what drove me in life? What do people think I was willing to die for? There is no way anyone who really heard and understood my message could turn me into the unique mediator between God and humans. I gave my heart and soul and ultimately my life to affirming God's presence with people. I preached the good news of a loving, utterly compassionate God, always ready to forgive. I lived and died for those beliefs. How ever could the Christian religion have come to proclaim to the world that God could not be present to people and would not forgive them unless I, a god-man savior, died on the cross for sinful humanity?!'"

"I guess if you were alive on earth today, you'd be angry or at least dismayed about what happened, but since you are now beyond human emotions like that, let me say I am angry for you. And I know I am not alone in being dismayed at how your humanity and your message have been distorted by the Christian religion. As I see it, the more people are upset by this the better, otherwise the man-god-savior-of-the-world theology about you will continue to dominate Christian thinking.

"But this raises another important question. If you are not the god-figure the Christian religion has always proclaimed you to be, why should Christians gather in memory of you?"

"I never imagined people gathering to sing my praises or to acknowledge me as someone different from them. I wanted my Jewish friends to remember me whenever they gathered to celebrate their history and their connection with God. It's the connection with God and how that plays out in people's lives that are important. Jews can focus on that; Muslims can focus on it also; people of any religion can do that. Christians should focus on it whenever they gather. And if in their gatherings Christians remember me as someone who dedicated his life to helping people see their connection with God, then my death will not have been in vain. I would like people to remember me for the message I gave my life for rather than falsely remembering and honoring me as a god-figure utterly different from every other human person."

"And if people remember you that way, they will surely appreciate that when you went off to a quiet place and prayed, your prayer would have been more like ours than they ever imagined. For decades I thought that being the divine Son of God gave you direct contact with your Father in heaven during your prayer. Now that I have come to know you as friend and companion I can appreciate that your prayer was nothing like that, but that it arose out of your human need to give voice to what was deepest in you.

"I wonder, though. Would you pray differently if you were alive on earth today?"

"There would be some difference. Like most Jews of my time I imagined that God demanded to be worshipped and wanted to be thanked. If I were human again, my prayer would reflect a more expansive understanding of God. I would not pray in the belief that God needs to hear from me or needs to be thanked, as if prayer is for God's sake. I would pray because I want to express gratitude for experiencing in a personal, human dimension the mystery of God. My prayer would express my joys, feelings, doubts, longings, pains, or whatever, as I live in the realization that I give human expression to this Ultimate Mystery we call God.

"I would liken prayer to singing when no one is present to hear the song. It's what is in the mind and heart of the singer that is important. Prayer need not be heard, but I'd want my prayer to give expression to thoughts, emotions and sentiments within me.

"In some ways, though, my prayer would not differ greatly from what I did when I lived in Galilee. I think prayer expresses a basic stance towards life and towards whatever and however we conceive God to be. I tried prayerfully to deepen my awareness of the utter graciousness of the God I humanly believed in, the God of my Jewish faith. I had no difficulty imagining God as a Gracious Being at work in the universe. I think the concept of graciousness would still be helpful, but not in terms of a heavenly Someone God being gracious. Rather it would be my awareness that I have been graced with the gift of life, the privilege of human consciousness, the blessing of experiencing love, and the beauty and the wonder of the natural world.

"Today you have a resource for prayer that we never had, your knowledge about the vastness of the universe and how it has unfolded. You can contemplate, as I was never humanly able to, the workings of a universe that brings the dust and gas of a star that exploded billions of years ago into human form. You can be aware of yourself as the universe finding a way to reflect on itself with conscious awareness. You can contemplate the reality that the power at work in the universe is in you. In other words, you have knowledge that should lead you into a profound sense of wonder, of privilege, and of gratitude for the magnificence and graciousness of the universe. You have knowledge that can lead you to appreciate that everything exists in the One, in God, and that in you, the One is given human expression.

"I would certainly use this information as the foundation of my prayer life because it provides the grateful stance towards life and God that I believe is at the heart of prayer. I would sit in wonder and contemplate what is behind the unfolding of the universe and how it all points to the Mystery we call God permeating everything. To be aware that I am part of this magnificent unfolding, and that it is all good, would be for me an experience of blessedness, of holiness, of communion with God. My prayer would consistently nurture and highlight the wonder of life and my desire to give it the best possible human expression I could."

"That sounds all very fine, but I can imagine many people would object that such an approach is escapist and too easy. It does not acknowledge the hardships of human experience. How can people who endure pain or sorrow have a profound sense of wonder and appreciation of the graciousness of life?"

"That was precisely the situation I came across when I was teaching. Life is hard for many people and you cannot expect them to embrace this style of prayer in difficult times. But you *can* try to teach them that God, however they think of God, is not the cause of their suffering. During my lifetime too many people believed that their burdens were intended by God. I tried to set people free from that understanding of God.

"I encouraged those who were dealing with illness or any sort of hardship to focus on the Spirit of God being with them, always, and to draw strength from that as they faced each day. That is not easy to do, as I found out for myself in the last days of my life. I would urge everyone, whatever the circumstances of their life, to believe in and draw strength from the Spirit and the power of God within them. Religion should constantly affirm that Presence in all people."

"It seems that Christianity is more concerned with praying to and worshipping a heavenly God than with affirming God's presence with people. What about worship? I've come to associate it with the concept of ancient gods who demanded fitting tribute and recognition. Is worship meaningful anymore?"

"Worship may fit with the concept of God in the Jewish and Christian Scriptures, but the reality of God I now know and experience has no need of worship. Whatever religious people do in their ceremonial gatherings they need to be aware that there is not a deity at the receiving end of their prayers, observing, listening, considering, responding and being grateful for their recognition."

"When I contrast the God you now know and experience with the notion of God in Scripture, I find myself using the all-pervasive and sustaining nature of the energy in the universe as a useful pointer to this Awesome Reality rather than the scriptural notion of a god who rules the world from heaven. Energy does not listen. It does not think the way we humans do. It has no need of our thanks or praise. It gets along very well without human prayer and worship. That helps me to understand that God has no need of worship, either.

"I prefer to use the word liturgy rather than worship. I think it highlights, or should highlight, that the religious ceremony is for the peoples' sake, not for God's sake."

"Yes, let people gather and let their gatherings resound with songs and prayers and gestures that proclaim God present in every person. Let the prayers constantly affirm the Divine Presence in everyone's life. And let the ritual of eating and drinking be a ritual of personal commitment to expressing that Presence in their daily lives. That's what I had in mind when I shared my last meal with my friends. It was about them making a commitment to keep my dream alive. That's what I would like to see in Christian liturgies."

"I find it lamentable that Roman Catholicism emphasizes worship of a heavenly God and dependence on a priestly caste which believes it alone has the power to bring God's presence to the people, as if God is not present to them already. When we begin to understand God and God's presence with us differently, the role of priesthood must surely change. What would you suggest?"

"I never wanted my apostles to be part of a priestly group. I was not a priest myself. What I looked for were leaders who would serve people by their lifestyle and teaching, and who would keep my dream of a better world alive. If there is to be a role in future Christianity for priests it should be closely modeled on my own example, practice and teaching. Priesthood should be grounded in the capacity to provide clear and faithful community leadership. Any priest should be answerable to the community for his or her ability to be a leader, capable of engaging religious faith with the contemporary worldview, willing and able to affirm the presence of God in everyone's' life, and courageous in challenging everyone to truly be neighbor. Any priest should be as on fire to establish the reign of God *on earth* as I was. In a religion that professes to follow my example, this should be standard practice with no exceptions."

"That's a tough job description."

"Would you leave something out?"

"Oh, no. It's just that there would be a mass exodus from priestly and episcopal ranks today if your expectations of Christian leadership were put into practice."

"Which simply means you have a dysfunctional Church that needs major reform."

"I don't want to spend time on that topic. We've been there often enough. I want to return to the potential for change in society.

"You said earlier you would like to live in these times with the knowledge we have available to us to expand our sense of wonder and appreciation about human existence and our intimate link with God. As you said, it is indeed wonderful, but when I look at western society, supposedly shaped by Christian values, the future looks bleak. Military expenditure vastly outweighs resources for the development of social and educational needs. Domestic and foreign economic policies are generally dictated by profit and greed. And it is not just the company directors who stand condemned by their policies and actions. Shareholders, many of whom would see themselves as solid Christian citizens, are more concerned with profit margins than with just dealings by the companies in which they invest.

Many politicians bow to the influence of lobbyists and the mega-rich and are dependent on their support for political survival. Their integrity is inevitably compromised by the quid pro quo situation pervasive in politics. The poor get poorer and the rich get richer. There is a growing suspicion of strangers with regard to immigration and assimilation. The institutional Church is considered irrelevant. The environment is being devastated. The media, which could be an incredible resource for human unity and development, are all too often profit-driven, divisive, and cater to the lowest common denominator of human intelligence. It's a sad, dismal picture."

"You should be thankful you didn't live two thousand years ago under the Romans! Most things you mention had their counterparts when I lived on earth. You are describing what I encountered. It was as sad and dismal then. And it looked just as hopeless.

"In the context of two thousand years of western Christian civilization, the situations you describe raise serious questions for the Christian religion. How, in the twenty-first century, is it possible that you can describe social, religious, political, and economic situations that would have made the Romans feel at home? I dreamed that my teaching would one day be put into practice in such a way that it would touch every level of society, would bring dignity to all people, would lessen violence, and would make God's reign visible on earth. Who or what had the opportunity and the duty to lead people to my message and help them implement it? Why hasn't the message to which I gave voice and which Christians affirm to be of God, been put into practice?

"Christian leadership needs to return to the vision of life I carried to my death as its priority if it is to be a relevant force for implementing social change. One of its major tasks is to preach the good news that every person, regardless of their race and religion, carries within them the presence and the power of the Mystery we call God. Only when that belief is nurtured can the presence and power of God in all people create a nobler, more compassionate, more just, human society. The kingdom of God cannot be realized on earth without that foundation.

"I believed firmly two thousand years ago that the Spirit of God would eventually win out over human stupidity, greed, and oppression. That Spirit is within and among you. Look around and see how it is present and how it is expressing itself. Clearly, the new consciousness you referred to earlier is dawning in the midst of the sad situation you just described. It's surfacing in the young, in people disenchanted with the formulas and rules of institutional religion, in business executives who want their businesses to operate on just and ethical principles. It's surfacing in parents and grandparents and teachers who want children to experience a better world. It's evident in people who care about the environment. It's alerting influential people that the current political, economic, ecclesial systems do not work for the betterment of humanity. Although it is broadly non-religious in nature, this consciousness could ultimately awaken religions to what they should be about. Whatever words people might use to describe it, this is the voice, the movement of God within the human community today. It must be listened to.

"I think it would be a privilege and a challenge to be human today, with the opportunity to participate in the dawning of this new consciousness. It provides an ideal opportunity to incorporate an understanding of God into the story of an unfolding universe and humanity's place in it. The resulting story could draw all humans together into a common appreciation of the dignity of human existence, a story to inspire all people to work together, as never before, to advance human development. It is a story that could bring an end to violence, domination, hatred and divisions. That story is yours to tell. You should tell it clearly and boldly.

"This is a decisive time for humanity and its future. Either you bring the exciting, uplifting and challenging possibilities of this new story to reality, or you settle for the sad and dismal future you outlined. I sincerely hope that with the vast resources available to it, humanity would do much better listening to the authentic voice of God speaking in and through people today than it has managed to do in the past two thousand years."

"Everything you have shared with me supports my long-held assumption that you wish to be remembered as someone who agonized over the human situation and how people, with the Spirit of God within them, could work together to create a better world."

"Yes. The Spirit of God moved me to see what humanity could become if people were helped to acknowledge, trust and follow the promptings of the same Spirit in them."

"I know the one Great Commandment featured large in your teaching, as it has for many other great religious teachers. I know you would insist still that loving our neighbor is the crucial test of whether anyone is a true follower of yours. But if you were here on earth today, is there anything else that you would highlight?"

"Yes, there is. It's obvious that human society in general operates on behavioral patterns that are out of step with the patterns of operation that govern the functioning of the universe. Basic to those patterns is the capacity to co-operate and for elements at all levels of reality to work with other elements to produce possibilities beyond their individual realities. The human species, as you well know, is the only life form on earth that can consciously refuse to co-operate. And you go further than that. You take up hard positions against one another. You do this at every level of human existence. You do it in your religions, in your politics, and in your social and economic systems. From any viewpoint you are a thoroughly divided and divisive life species.

"The only path out of antagonism, condemnation, violence and warfare is compassion, tolerance and respect. People of religious faith should readily follow that path, motivated both by the dignity of all humans and by the conviction that everyone and everything exists in the reality of the one God. As I said earlier, the fate of humanity is in your hands, not God's. You know what needs to be done and you know how to do it."

"We do. If only we Christians remember you as you clearly want to be remembered, there is hope for Christianity and the future of humanity."

"Yes. Remember me for the right reasons!"

"I'll do my best to spread the word… Thanks, Jesus, it's so good to talk with you."

"Isn't that what friends are for? Shalom, Michael. I'm always with you, my friend."

More titles by Michael Morwood - available in paperback editions.

Tomorrow's Catholic. Understanding God and Jesus in a New Millennium 1997. USA edition: Twenty-Third Publications. Mystic, CT. Australian edition: Spectrum Publications, Richmond, Vic. Australia

> I was reminded of a book that shook the foundations of Christianity back in 1963. *Honest to God*, by Anglican Bishop John A. T. Robinson was a radical work, radical in the sense that it got to the roots of belief and practice, unafraid to discuss the most sacrosanct, inviolable subjects. It was, like this book, a very readable small work, requiring no great theological mind to understand what the author was getting at. Modest as it was, it contained gems of wisdom that resonated beautifully with what many hearts were thinking at the time. *Tomorrow's Catholic* is another such gem that will not go unnoticed because it is meant for ordinary people, struggling to make sense of a religion increasingly out of touch with people's lives, beliefs, desires and expectations.
> - Eugene H. Ciarlo, book editor for *The American Catholic*

Is Jesus God? Finding Our Faith. 2001 USA edition: Crossroad Publishing Company. NY. Australian edition: Spectrum Publications.

> A provocative, powerful and life-giving book! Michael Morwood is raising the right and obvious questions that all Christians must face. In his response he provides fresh and perceptive possibilities for a modern and relevant faith.
> - Bishop John Shelby Spong

This is the book I have been waiting for... Everyone I know who has read this book appreciates its premise and applauds its author.
- *National Catholic Reporter* review 10th August 2001

Praying a New Story. 2004 USA edition: Orbis Books, Maryknoll. NY.

Award Winner, Best Spiritual Books, *Spirituality & Health Awards 2004:*

Invigorating, poetic and imaginative... the perfect resource for small groups interested in exploring new avenues of devotion and spiritual practice.

From Sand to Solid Ground. Questions of Faith for Modern Christians. 2007. USA edition: Crossroad Publishing Company. NY.

The work responds to the need of contemporary Christians to understand their faith in a new way which respects their secular world-view and enables them to believe in Christ and believe in themselves and our place in the universe. Morwood's style is direct and challenging yet compassionate and reassuring. Christians who are looking for a 21st century handle for their faith will be rewarded by their effort to read this important work.
- *USA Catholic Press Awards 2008*, 3rd place: Education:

From Sand to Solid Ground is an extraordinary book of courage and vision. Michael Morwood dares to speak and articulate clearly what more and more Catholics today quietly struggle with and question. His writing exemplifies the giftedness of a true teacher. The book's simple yet elegant style succeeds where perhaps more scholarly, academic theology does not. True teaching not only exposes and explains but inspires and explores as well. Morwood's passionate approach to the faith does all of this and more.

- Barbara Fiand, author of *From Religion Back to Faith* and *In the Stillness You Will Know*.

Children Praying a New Story. A Resource for Parents, Grandparents and Teachers. 2009. Kelmor Publishing. South Bend. Indiana.

This is not a book for children. It is a resource for educators and for any adult Christian seeking to deepen understanding of faith in light of the "new story" of the universe and the development of life on earth. The book responds to adult questions such as: How do we now think about, understand or teach Christmas or Easter or Pentecost? How do we pray? How might we pray with young children at home or in a classroom? How can we use gospel stories about Jesus? How do "sacraments" fit into the new story?

If you are a parent, grandparent or teacher our role is not to introduce our children, grandchildren or students into our faith or our parents' faith. As a sixty seven year old Liverpool-Irish-Canadian-Catholic the Catholic Church today is radically different from the church into which I was baptized over a font in St. James, Bootle, in 1942.

It is a different church and a different faith for my children and hopefully for my grandchildren. Michael Morwood, in responding to the questions and faith struggles of adults, many of them parents, grandparents and teachers, has given us a way to introduce God and Jesus to future generations for whom the new story is as familiar as multiplication tables were to us.
- John Quinn, Editor, *NewCatholicTimes,* Canada. October 19, 2009

*God Is Near. Understanding a Changing Church. 1991. Australian edition. Spectrum Publications, Richmond, Vic. Australia, is no longer in print. USA edition, 2002, **God Is Near: Trusting Our Faith**, Crossroad Publishing Company. NY.*

Faith, Hope and a Bird Called George. A Spiritual Fable. 2011 USA edition: Twenty-Third Publications, New London. Ct. Australian edition: John Garratt Publishing, Mulgrave. Vic.

Morwood's enchanting little tome follows the theological quest of Faith, a mature woman in both years and theology who is approaching the final stages of her life and seeks a deeper understanding of what it means to be in relationship with God. No longer content with traditional religious answers, Faith wonders what to do now that she has expanded her understanding of the nature of the Divine beyond the Father-Sky-God toward a panentheistic understanding of God as the "ground of our Being". During conversations with her cat named Hope and her bird named George, Faith comes to a deeper awareness of her place in the cosmos. With gentle humour and piercing inquisitiveness Faith is encouraged by her curious cat Hope to debate her bird George whose previous owner was a member of the clergy. George's traditional answers fail to satisfy and as Faith tries to interpret their meaning for her doubting cat, she finds herself moving to a new way of being in the world.

If you find yourself on a journey that sees you questioning traditional interpretations of Christianity, this book will make an excellent companion. Only, be sure to by a couple of copies, for you are sure to want to give it to friends. If you are clergy you'll just have to buy dozens of copies because this is one of those books you're going to want to give to all those folks who you encounter who are searching for an approach to faith that does not require them to suspend their understanding of reality in order to trust that God does indeed dwell in, with and through us.

- Pastor Dawn Hutchins, Newmarket, Canada

It's Time. Challenges to the Doctrine of the Faith. Kelmor Publishing. 2013

"If this book doesn't make you think about what you truly believe nothing will. It's a book to challenge, and paradixocially strengthen, the very foundations of your faith!"
- Brian Coyne. Editor, *Catholica*

For articles and other information:
http://www.morwood.org

Made in the USA
San Bernardino, CA
07 May 2014